SCIENTISTS
AND
INVENTORS
OF THE
RENAISSANCE

SCIENTISTS
AND
INVENTORS
OF THE
RENAISSANCE

Edited by Robert Curley, Senior Editor, Science and Technology

Britannica
Educational Publishing

IN ASSOCIATION WITH

ROSEN
EDUCATIONAL SERVICES

Published in 2013 by Britannica Educational Publishing
(a trademark of Encyclopædia Britannica, Inc.) in association with Rosen Educational
Services, LLC

29 East 21st Street, New York, NY 10010.

Distributed exclusively by Rosen Educational Services.
For a listing of additional Britannica Educational Publishing titles, call toll free (800) 237-9932.

First Edition

Britannica Educational Publishing
J.E. Luebering: Senior Manager
Marilyn L. Barton: Senior Coordinator, Production Control
Steven Bosco: Director, Editorial Technologies
Lisa S. Braucher: Senior Producer and Data Editor
Yvette Charboneau: Senior Copy Editor
Kathy Nakamura: Manager, Media Acquisition
Robert Curley, Senior Editor, Science and Technology

Rosen Educational Services
Jeanne Nagle: Senior Editor
Nelson Sá: Art Director
Cindy Reiman: Photography Manager
Brian Garvey: Designer, Cover Design
Introduction by Richard Barrington

Library of Congress Cataloging-in-Publication Data

Scientists and inventors of the Renaissance/edited by Robert Curley. — First edition.
    pages cm. — (The Renaissance)
"In association with Britannica Educational Publishing, Rosen Educational Services."
Includes bibliographical references and index.
ISBN 978-1-61530-880-4 (library binding)
1. Science, Renaissance. 2. Scientists — Europe — History — 17th century. 3. Inventors —
Europe — History — 17th century. 4. Science — Europe — History — 17th century. I. Curley,
Robert, 1955– editor.
Q125.2.R456 2013
500.92'24 — dc23

                                                                    2012020369

Manufactured in the United States of America

On the cover, p. iii : Sir Isaac Newton. Science & Society Picture Library/Getty Images

Cover (background pattern), pp. i, iii, 1, 35, 73, 98, 136, 155, 156, 158, 161 © iStockphoto.com/
fotozambra; p. x (sun) Hemera/Thinkstock; remaining interior graphic elements
©iStockphoto.com/Petr Babkin

CONTENTS

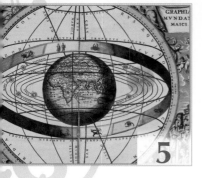

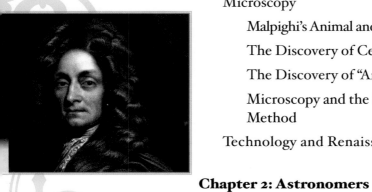

Introduction   x

Chapter 1: The Scientific Revolution   1

Astronomy   3

   The Ptolemaic Inheritance   4

   The New Sun-Centred System   6

Mechanics   9

   Galileo and Descartes on Motion   10

   Newton's Laws   12

Optics   15

Chemistry   17

   The Royal Society of London   18

Medicine   20

   The Anatomists   21

   The Futile Search for an Easy
   System   24

   Harvey and the Experimental
   Method   26

Microscopy   27

   Malpighi's Animal and Plant Studies   28

   The Discovery of Cells   29

   The Discovery of "Animalcules"   30

   Microscopy and the Scientific
   Method   32

Technology and Renaissance Science   32

Chapter 2: Astronomers   35

Nicolaus Copernicus   35

Early Life and Education 37
Copernicus's Astronomical Work 39
Publication of *De Revolutionibus* 43
Tycho Brahe 44
Youth and Education 44
Mature Career 48
Johannes Kepler 49
Kepler's Social World 51
Astronomical Work 52
Galileo 59
Refracting and Reflecting Telescopes 60
Early Life and Career 62
Telescopic Discoveries 64
Galileo's Copernicanism 66
Galileo and the Inquisition 70

Chapter 3: Natural Philosophers 73
René Descartes 73
Early Life and Education 74
Residence in the Netherlands 76
The World, The Discourse on Method, and *The Meditations* 77
Physics, Physiology, and Morals 78
Final Years 80
Isaac Newton 81
Formative Influences 81
Early Work on Motion 83
The *Principia* 84
Newton's Final Years 86
Christiaan Huygens 87

36

47

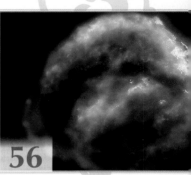

56

Robert Boyle 91
   Early Life and Education 91
   Scientific Career 92
   Discovering Boyle's Law 94
   Theological Activities 96
   Mature Years in London 97

Chapter 4: Anatomists, Physicians, and Microscopists 98
Mondino Dei Liucci 98
Paracelsus 99
   Education 99
   Career 100
   Contributions to Medicine 103
Girolamo Fracastoro 104
Ambroise Paré 105
Andreas Vesalius 106
   Education 106
   The *Fabrica* 107
   Career 109
   Assessment 110
Gabriel Fallopius 110
Hieronymus Fabricius 111
Santorio Santorio 112
William Harvey 113
   Education and Career 113
   Physician to the King 114
   Later Life 116
   Discovery of Circulation 116
   The Invention of the Microscope 117

Jan Baptista van Helmont   121

   Education and Early Life   121

   Publications   122

   Major Experiments   122

   Other Contributions   123

Giovanni Alfonso Borelli   124

Franciscus Sylvius   124

Marcello Malpighi   126

   Life   126

   Assessment   130

Thomas Willis   130

Robert Hooke   131

Antonie van Leeuwenhoek   132

Chapter 5: Inventors   **136**

Johannes Gutenberg   136

   Life   137

   Invention of the Press   137

   Printing of the Bible   139

Hans Lippershey   141

   Sir John Harington and the Flush Toilet   142

Cornelis Drebbel   142

Evangelista Torricelli   143

Otto von Guericke   144

Giuseppe Campani   147

James Gregory   148

Denis Papin   150

Thomas Savery   152

Conclusion   155

Glossary   156

INTRODUCTION

The journey humankind took from a superstitious to a scientific understanding of the physical world was a long one. The Renaissance was a critical period in the course of this journey, as scientists began developing not just a more enlightened view of the world, but also principles and methods that would guide future generations in expanding their scientific knowledge. At the same time, Renaissance inventors figured out new ways to harness the power of the physical world to vastly increase the capacity for human accomplishment.

This period of science and invention does not solely consist of facts and formulas. It is also a story about personalities with the inspiration and courage to look outside the narrow scope of the established body of knowledge. At the time, this curiosity was often considered bold to the point of defiance, and could carry the risk of severe punishment. This type of conflict adds drama to the story of Renaissance scientists and inventors, and makes their achievements all the more remarkable.

The scientific revolution of the 15th-17th centuries was not just a series of isolated breakthroughs, but a clear change in the method and adventurousness of scientific thinking. As a result, science became a distinct discipline, after having been considered up to that point as simply an offshoot of philosophy. Consistent with this redefinition, science became more concerned with understanding how things worked than with debating why they worked the way they did.

This concept was revolutionary in that it challenged two established orders. One was the authority of the Roman Catholic Church, which was already going through a period of upheaval with the Protestant Reformation. The scientific revolution also took aim at the body of scientific knowledge that had been established by classical Greek thinkers nearly 2,000 years earlier, and which had been more or less universally accepted since.

This movement was also revolutionary in its scope, as it swept across several disciplines of science, including astronomy, physics, chemistry, anatomy, medicine, and biology. All these fields saw new theories that were usually argued over and, often, subsequently refuted and refined. The scientists who advanced these theories may have been persecuted in their own time, only to be celebrated and respected from the perspective of history. The process was neither easy for the individuals leading the scientific revolution nor universally welcomed by a society that frequently balked at proposed new ways of thinking about the world. In the end, however, science was forever changed. Man gained a new empowerment to try to affect the physical world and use it to his advantage.

Each of the fields listed above can trace its modern roots back to the scientific revolution, and this is especially true with the field of astronomy. One indication of how much astronomy changed during the scientific revolution is that when the period began, astronomy was closely related to what is now known as astrology. The movements of stars and planets were tracked to some degree, but largely as the basis for predicting the futures of leading citizens rather than to foster an understanding

The ancient astronomer Ptolemy, observing the stars using a quadrant and with the aid of a muse. Photos.com/Thinkstock

of the forces behind those movements. Indeed, one of the scientific revolution's earliest major figures, Copernicus, got his start assisting with the production of astrological forecasts. However, as he tracked the movement of the heavenly bodies, Copernicus increasingly turned his attention to formulating an explanation for those movements. This ultimately led to his advancement of the heliocentric theory, which held that the Sun rather than Earth was at the centre of planetary movement.

The theories of Copernicus were flawed, but they created a foundation for subsequent improvement and advancement. Tycho Brahe, who followed Copernicus, was sparked toward an interest in astronomy when, as a young boy, he witnessed an eclipse of the Sun. It is significant that Brahe's career should start with witnessing an astronomical event, since his major contribution to the field was the vast collection of precise celestial observations he made in the latter half of the 16th century. These observations led Brahe to the conclusion that the Copernican model of the universe was often inaccurate. Brahe himself never came up with a fully satisfactory model, but his carefully documented observations created a wealth of data for future astronomers to analyze.

One beneficiary of Brahe's work was Johannes Kepler, who had been invited to work with Brahe and inherited his mentor's rich catalogue of planetary observations. Ultimately, Kepler discovered three important laws of planetary movement, including the assertion that the planets' orbits followed an elliptical course around the Sun. As he worked toward understanding the dynamics driving the movement of planets, Kepler helped lay the groundwork for the later understanding of gravity. Because of this and his writings on the behaviour of light, Kepler is a significant figure in the history of physics as well as astronomy.

Another scientist that had a foothold in these two fields was Galileo Galilei. Galileo is remembered for many things, including his refinements to the making of telescopes, which enabled many new astronomical discoveries, and his mathematical approach to the study of motion. In the process of developing his great body of work, Galileo was highly influential in formulating the scientific method, a process of discovery through systematic experimentation, observation, and calculation.

Unfortunately, not everyone in the 17th century was ready for a logical rather than a doctrinal view of the universe, especially when it conflicted with passages from the Bible and traditional church teachings. As a result, Galileo ran afoul of the papal inquisition, which slowed but did not stop his work later in life. By the time he died in 1642, Galileo had left behind a group of theories that addressed not only the movement of planets and stars, but also physical properties of light and objects on Earth.

The Renaissance astronomers who started by seeking to better explain movements in the heavens set the stage for a clearer understanding of the physical world here on Earth. This examination of the physical world evolved into the modern field of physics. A number of figures from the scientific revolution were instrumental in formalizing and furthering the study of physics. René Descartes, for example, is best known today as a philosopher, but like many of his peers he epitomized the expression "renaissance man" by making a mark in several fields, including anatomy and physics. Descartes believed that all things — including organisms — behaved according to mechanical principles, and that their actions were interrelated with and influenced by those of other entities. These are rather general principles, but they do fit with a modern understanding of the physical world.

Another contributor along these same lines was Christiaan Huygens, who formulated mathematical explanations for principles of complex motion such as the oscillation of a pendulum and centrifugal force. Huygens was a 17th century contemporary of Descartes who directly exchanged ideas with the French philosopher. In Isaac Newton, the late Renaissance period produced a scientist whose work represents the fundamental basis of modern physics. His work on the composition of white light remains essential to the field of optics, just as his three laws of motion and his law of universal gravitation have helped make mechanics measurable and predictable.

The formalization of science as a discipline also was seen in the field of chemistry, which developed over the course of the scientific revolution from the mystical realm of alchemy to a collection of demonstrable properties and principles. This progression took place relatively late in the Renaissance, as chemistry came to benefit from many of the mechanical principles that had been established. Robert Boyle, for example, maintained that chemical properties had mechanical explanations, and he devised laboratory procedures to help demonstrate this.

In addition to the formalization of experimental methods, a recurring theme in the scientific revolution is the interrelation of different fields of science. Good examples of this can be seen in anatomy and medicine. The two are naturally related to one another, but other sciences also influenced these fields. The study of mechanical principles helped spur the quest for an understanding of how the body operates as a mechanism. Also, developments in lenses and optics were critical to the microscopic study of biology, which, in turn, was essential to anatomy and medicine. Meanwhile, in the first half of the 16th century, Paracelsus established that chemistry played a role in the operation of the human body, a principle fundamental to the development of modern medicine.

Not only did anatomy and medicine benefit from the contributions of related disciplines, but as was so often the case during the scientific revolution, these fields progressed because contemporaries working on the same problems were able to build on one another's work. Thus, in the 16th and 17th centuries a line can be drawn connecting the anatomical studies of Andreas Vesalius, Gabriel Fallopius, and Hieronymus Fabricius, culminating in William Harvey's publication of a comprehensive explanation for how blood circulates throughout the human body.

Harvey is a prime example of how Renaissance scientists were not always left to work in peace. Staunchly loyal to the British monarchy, Harvey was sidetracked by the English Civil War, and he was forced to live in exile for a time. Despite this and other setbacks, such as the Great Fire of London, Harvey's work in the circulatory system stands as one of the pivotal achievements of Renaissance anatomy, one that was critical to subsequent advancements in surgery.

Overall, medicine progressed from a science wrought with superstition and often barbaric practices to the beginnings of a modern understanding of the human body. This journey was a long and slow one, but the application of the scientific method during the Renaissance can be credited with starting the field of medicine down this path.

With Renaissance scientists having made bold advances across such a wide range of fields, the inevitable question was what would mankind do with this new and exciting knowledge? A number of the era's inventors soon provided the answers to that question. Applying both the new knowledge and active curiosity of the era, Renaissance inventors produced innovations as diverse as the submarine, barometer, air pump, electric generator, pressure cooker, steam engine, and even an early version of a flushing toilet.

An improved understanding of science helped facilitate these new inventions, but many inventions also served the advancement of science. For example, the telescope was vital to astronomy, just as the microscope was to biology and medicine. The printing press played a key role in the flowering of the sciences during the Renaissance, as it allowed far-flung scientists to learn from each other's successes and failures, and take the next step toward progress.

At the time, the scientific revolution may not have seemed so revolutionary. After all, the discoveries and inventions of the Renaissance played out over the course of three centuries, so to scientists of the era, progress may have seemed slow and sporadic. Much of the work during the scientific revolution can be described as an incremental process of getting closer to the truth. In a sense, though, the often arduous path taken toward realizing these collective achievements makes them even more impressive. Viewed from the perspective of history, the changes in scientific knowledge and methodology that took place during the Renaissance do indeed seem revolutionary. In fact, it is impossible to imagine the modern world without these advances.

The Scientific Revolution

According to medieval scientists, matter was composed of four elements—earth, air, fire, and water—and combinations of these elements made up the world of visible objects. The cosmos, consisting of Earth and all the heavenly bodies, was a series of concentric spheres in motion, the farther ones carrying the stars around in their daily courses. At the centre was the globe of Earth, heavy and static. Motion was either perfectly circular, as in the heavens, or, as on Earth, irregular and naturally downward. Earth had three landmasses—Europe, Asia, and Africa—and was unknown and uninhabitable in its southern zones. Human beings, the object of all creation, were composed of four humours—black and yellow bile, blood, and phlegm—and the body's health was determined by the relative proportions of each humour. The cosmos was alive with a universal consciousness with which people could interact in various ways, and the heavenly bodies were generally believed to influence human character and events.

These views were an amalgam of thought inherited from the Greeks and Romans and continued by the Christian church. From what can be inferred from written sources, they shaped the way even educated people in Europe experienced and interpreted phenomena. What was understood about nature by Europeans who did not

Artist's interpretation of the four humours (clockwise from top left): *phlegmatic (phlem; sluggish), sanguine (blood; cheerful), melancholic (black bile; gloomy or depressed), and choleric (yellow bile; easily angered).* NYPL/Science Source/Photo Researchers/Getty Images

read or write books is more difficult to tell, except that belief in magic, good and evil spirits, witchcraft, and forecasting the future was universal. The church preferred that Christians seek their well-being through faith, the sacraments, and the intercession of the saints and Mary, the mother of Jesus, but in fact most clergy shared the common beliefs in occult forces and lent their authority to them.

Among at least the formally educated, if not among the general population, this entire system of scientific thought underwent a revolution during the Renaissance of the 15th, 16th, and 17th centuries. A new view of nature emerged, replacing the Greek view that had dominated science for almost 2,000 years. Science became an autonomous discipline, distinct from both philosophy and technology, and it came to be regarded as having utilitarian goals. Out of the ferment of this period there arose a number of transformations: (1) the reeducation of common sense in favour of abstract reasoning; (2) the substitution of a quantitative for a qualitative view of nature; (3) the view of nature as a machine rather than as an organism; (4) the development of an experimental method that sought definite answers to certain limited questions couched in the framework of specific theories; and (5) the acceptance of new criteria for explanation, stressing the "how" rather than the "why" that had characterized the medieval search for final causes. By the end of the Renaissance, it may not be too much to say that science had replaced Christianity as the focal point of European civilization.

ASTRONOMY

The scientific revolution began in astronomy. Medieval astronomy was dominated by the assumption that Earth was at the centre of the universe. The supreme description of this geocentric, or Earth-centred, system was that of the Alexandrian astronomer and mathematician Ptolemy (2nd century CE). The Ptolemaic system was generally accepted until Earth was displaced from the centre of the universe in the 16th and 17th centuries by the Copernican system and by Kepler's laws of planetary motion.

THE PTOLEMAIC INHERITANCE

Believing that the order of the cosmos is fundamentally mathematical, the Greeks held that it is possible to discover the harmonies of the universe by contemplating the regular motions of the heavens. The "natural" expectation of such a world view was that the heavenly bodies (Sun, Moon, planets, and stars) must travel in uniform motion along the most "perfect" path possible—that is, a circle. Indeed, Plato, in the 4th century BCE, is reported to have instructed astronomers to develop predictively accurate theories using only combinations of uniform circular motion.

In fact, however, the paths of the Sun, Moon, and planets as observed from Earth are not circular. Ptolemy explained this "imperfection" by postulating eccentric motion: the apparently irregular movements were a combination of several regular circular motions seen in perspective from a stationary Earth. A body travelling at uniform speed on a circular path with Earth at its centre will sweep out equal angles in equal times from a terrestrial perspective. However, if the path's centre is displaced from Earth, the body will sweep out equal angles in unequal times (again, from a terrestrial perspective), moving slowest when farthest from Earth (apogee) and fastest when nearest Earth (perigee). With this simple eccentric model Ptolemy explained the Sun's varying motion through the zodiac.

In order to explain the motion of the planets, Ptolemy combined eccentricity with an epicyclic model. In the Ptolemaic system each planet revolves uniformly around a small circular path (the epicycle), and this small circular path itself revolves around Earth along a larger circular path (the deferent). Because one half of an epicycle runs counter to the general motion of the deferent path, the combined motion will sometimes make it appear that a

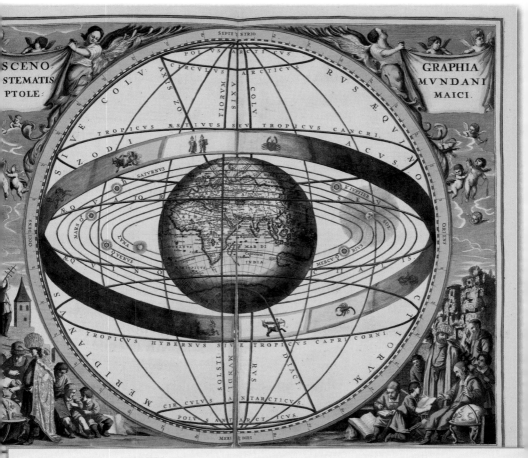

Illustration representing Ptolemy's geocentric system of the universe. DEA/G. Cigolini/Veneranda Biblioteca Ambrosiana/De Agostini/Getty Images

planet slows down or even reverses direction (retrogrades). By carefully coordinating these two cycles, the epicyclic model explained the observed phenomenon that planets retrograde when at perigee.

Ptolemy believed that the heavenly bodies' circular motions were caused by their being attached to unseen revolving solid spheres. For example, an epicycle would be the "equator" of a spinning sphere lodged in the space between two spherical shells surrounding Earth. He discovered that if he represented the motions of the Sun, the Moon, and the five known planets with spheres, he could nest them inside one another with no empty space left over and in such a manner that the solar and lunar distances agreed with his calculations.

Ptolemy's theory generally fitted the data available to him with a good degree of accuracy, and his book, the *Almagest*, became the vehicle by which Greek astronomy was transmitted to astronomers of the Middle Ages and Renaissance. It essentially molded astronomy for the next millennium and a half.

THE NEW SUN-CENTRED SYSTEM

Although there had been earlier discussions of the possibility that Earth actually moved through the cosmos, the Ptolemaic system persisted, with minor adjustments, into the 16th century. Polish astronomer Nicolaus Copernicus was the first to propound a comprehensive heliocentric, or Sun-centred, theory, equal in scope and predictive capability to Ptolemy's geocentric system. Relying on virtually the same data as Ptolemy had possessed, Copernicus turned the universe inside out, putting the Sun at the centre and setting Earth into motion around it. Copernicus's theory, published in 1543, possessed a qualitative simplicity that Ptolemaic astronomy appeared to lack.

The reception of Copernican astronomy amounted to victory by infiltration. Large-scale opposition to the theory eventually developed in the church and elsewhere, but by that time most of the best professional astronomers had found some aspect or other of the new system indispensable. Copernicus's book *De revolutionibus orbium coelestium libri VI* ("Six Books Concerning the Revolutions of the Heavenly Orbs"), published in 1543, became a standard reference for advanced problems in astronomical research, particularly for its mathematical techniques. Thus, it was widely read by mathematical astronomers, in spite of its central hypothesis that the Sun was at the centre of the cosmos, which was widely ignored.

During the 16th century the Danish astronomer Tycho Brahe rejected both the old Ptolemaic and the new Copernican systems. However, because he was responsible for major changes in observation, he unwittingly provided the data that ultimately decided the argument in favour of the new astronomy. Using larger, stabler, and better calibrated instruments, Tycho observed regularly over extended periods, thereby obtaining a continuity of observations that were accurate for planets to within about one minute of arc—several times better than any previous observation. Several of Tycho's observations contradicted accepted wisdom. For example, a nova that appeared in 1572 exhibited no parallax (meaning that it lay at a very great distance) and was thus not of the sublunary sphere and therefore contradicted the old assertion that the heavens were immutable. Similarly, a succession of comets appeared to be moving freely through a region that was supposed to be filled with solid, crystalline spheres.

To avoid various undesirable implications of the Ptolemaic and Copernican systems, Tycho devised his own world system. He retained from the ancient Ptolemaic system the idea of Earth as a fixed centre of the universe around which the Sun and Moon revolved, but he held that, as in the newer system of Copernicus, all other planets revolved around the Sun. As in both the Tychonic and the Ptolemaic systems, Tycho believed that an outer sphere containing the fixed stars revolved every day around Earth.

At the beginning of the 17th century, the German astronomer Johannes Kepler placed the Copernican hypothesis on firm astronomical footing. Converted to the new astronomy as a student and deeply motivated by a desire to find the mathematical principles of order and harmony according to which God had constructed the world, Kepler spent his life looking for simple mathematical relationships that described planetary motions. His painstaking search for the real order of the universe forced him finally to abandon the Platonic ideal of uniform circular motion in his search for a physical basis for the motions of the heavens.

In 1609 Kepler announced two new planetary laws derived from Tycho's data: (1) the planets travel around the Sun in elliptical orbits, one focus of the ellipse being occupied by the Sun; and (2) a planet moves in its orbit in such a manner that a line drawn from the planet to the Sun always sweeps out equal areas in equal times. With these two laws, Kepler abandoned uniform circular motion of the planets on their spheres, thus raising the fundamental physical question of what holds the planets in their orbits. He attempted to provide a physical basis for the planetary motions by means of a force analogous to the magnetic force, the qualitative properties of which had been recently described in England by William Gilbert in his influential treatise, *De Magnete, Magneticisque Corporibus et de Magno Magnete Tellure* (1600; "On the Magnet, Magnetic Bodies, and the Great Magnet of the Earth"). The impending marriage of astronomy and physics had been announced.

In 1618 Kepler stated his third law, which was one of many laws concerned with the harmonies of the planetary motions: (3) the square of the period in which a planet orbits the Sun is proportional to the cube of its mean distance from the Sun.

A powerful blow was dealt to traditional cosmology by the Italian Galileo Galilei, who early in the 17th century used the telescope, a recent invention of Dutch lens grinders, to look toward the heavens. In 1610 Galileo announced observations that contradicted many traditional cosmological assumptions. He observed that the Moon is not a smooth, polished surface, as had been claimed since the days of the Greeks, but that it is jagged and mountainous. Earthshine on the Moon revealed that Earth, like the other planets, shines by reflected light. Like Earth, Jupiter was observed to have satellites; hence, Earth had been demoted from its unique position. The phases of Venus proved that planet orbits the Sun, not Earth. Most stunning of all, the Milky Way was composed of countless stars whose existence no one had suspected until Galileo saw them. Here were observations that struck at the very roots of established thought.

MECHANICS

The battle for Copernicanism was fought in the realm of mechanics as well as astronomy. Here the new thinkers had to deal with the long-accepted physics of the Greek philosopher Aristotle, who was primarily concerned with the philosophical question of the nature of motion as one variety of change. Aristotle assumed that a constant motion requires a constant cause; that is to say, as long as a body remains in motion, a force must be acting on that body. He considered the motion of a body through a resisting medium as proportional to the force producing the motion and inversely proportional to the resistance of the medium. Aristotle used this relationship to argue against the existence of a void, for in a void resistance is zero, and the relationship loses meaning.

Aristotle also considered the cosmos to be divided into two qualitatively different realms, governed by two different kinds of laws. In the terrestrial realm, within the sphere of the Moon, rectilinear up-and-down motion is characteristic. Heavy bodies, by their nature, seek the centre and tend to move downward in a natural motion. Light bodies, in direct contrast, move naturally upward. In the celestial realm, on the other hand, uniform circular motion is natural, thus producing the motions of the heavenly bodies.

Thus the entire Ptolemaic-Aristotelian system inherited from the Greeks and perpetuated by the universities stood or fell as a monolith, for it rested on the idea of Earth's fixity at the centre of the cosmos. Removing Earth from the centre destroyed the doctrine of natural motion and place, and circular motion of Earth was incompatible with Aristotelian physics.

GALILEO AND DESCARTES ON MOTION

Galileo contributed to the science of mechanics as well as astronomy, and in so doing he developed the foundations for a new physics that was both highly mathematizable and directly related to the problems facing the new cosmology. Galileo attacked the problems of Earth's rotation and its revolution by logical analysis. Interested in finding the natural acceleration of falling bodies, he was able to derive the law of free fall (the distance, s, varies as the square of the time, t^2). Combining this result with a rudimentary form of the principle of inertia, he was able to derive the parabolic path of projectile motion. Furthermore, his principle of inertia enabled him to meet the traditional physical objections to Earth's motion: since a body in motion tends to remain in motion, projectiles and other objects on the terrestrial surface will tend to share the motions of Earth, which will thus be imperceptible to someone standing on Earth. For this reason, bodies fall to the base of towers from which they are dropped (since they share with the tower the rotation of Earth), just as a ball dropped from the top of a mast of a moving ship falls to the base of the mast (since it shares with the mast the forward motion of the ship). If the ball were allowed to move on a frictionless horizontal plane, it would continue to move forever. Hence, Galileo concluded, the planets, once set in circular motion, continue to move in circles forever.

The 17th-century contributions to mechanics of the French philosopher René Descartes, like his contributions to the scientific endeavour as a whole, were more concerned with problems in the foundations of science than with the solution of specific technical problems. He was principally concerned with the conceptions of matter and motion as part of his general program for science—namely, to explain all the phenomena of nature in terms of matter and motion. This program, known as the mechanical philosophy, came to be the dominant theme of 17th-century science.

Descartes rejected the idea that one piece of matter could act on another through empty space; instead, forces must be propagated by a material substance, the "ether," that fills all space. Bodies once in motion, Descartes argued, remain in motion in a straight line unless and until they are deflected from this line by the impact of another body. All changes of motion are the result of such impacts. Hence, the ball falls at the foot of the mast because, unless struck by another body, it continues to move with the ship. Planets move around the Sun because they are swept around by whirlpools of the ether filling all space.

According to Descartes, all natural phenomena depend on the collisions of small particles, and so it is of great importance to discover the quantitative laws of impact. This was done by Descartes's disciple, the Dutch physicist Christiaan Huygens, who formulated the laws of conservation of momentum and of kinetic energy (the latter being valid only for elastic collisions).

NEWTON'S LAWS

The work of Isaac Newton represents the culmination of the scientific revolution at the end of the 17th century. His monumental *Philosophiae Naturalis Principia Mathematica* (1687; *Mathematical Principles of Natural Philosophy*), known simply as the *Principia*, solved the major problems posed by the scientific revolution in mechanics and in cosmology. It provided a physical basis for Kepler's laws, unified celestial and terrestrial physics under one set of laws, and established the problems and methods that dominated much of astronomy and physics for well over a century. By means of the concept of force, Newton was able to synthesize two important components of the scientific revolution, the mechanical philosophy and the mathematization of nature.

Newton was able to derive all these striking results from his three laws of motion:

1. Every body continues in its state of rest or of motion in a straight line unless it is compelled to change that state by force impressed on it;
2. The change of motion is proportional to the motive force impressed and is made in the

The title page of Philosophiae Naturalis Principia Mathematica, *Isaac Newton's masterpiece and one of most the defining scientific works ever published.* Daniel Berehulak/Getty Images

        direction of the straight line in which that
        force is impressed;

3.   To every action there is always opposed an
        equal reaction: or, the mutual actions of two
        bodies upon each other are always equal.

The second law was put into its modern form $F = ma$ (where a is acceleration) by the Swiss mathematician Leonhard Euler in 1750. In this form, it is clear that the rate of change of velocity is directly proportional to the force acting on a body and inversely proportional to its mass.

In order to apply his laws to astronomy, Newton had to extend the mechanical philosophy beyond the limits set by Descartes. He postulated a gravitational force acting between any two objects in the universe, even though he was unable to explain how this force could be propagated.

By means of his laws of motion and a gravitational force proportional to the inverse square of the distance between the centres of two bodies, Newton could deduce Kepler's laws of planetary motion. Galileo's law of free fall is also consistent with Newton's laws. The same force that causes objects to fall near the surface of Earth also holds the Moon and planets in their orbits.

Newton's physics led to the conclusion that the shape of Earth is not precisely spherical but should bulge at the Equator. The confirmation of this prediction by French expeditions in the mid-18th century helped persuade most European scientists to change from Cartesian to Newtonian physics. Newton also used the nonspherical shape of Earth to explain the precession of the equinoxes, using the differential action of the Moon and Sun on the equatorial bulge to show how the axis of rotation would change its direction.

OPTICS

The science of optics in the 17th century expressed the fundamental outlook of the scientific revolution by combining an experimental approach with a quantitative analysis of phenomena. Optics had its origins in Greece, especially in the works of Euclid (c. 300 BCE), who stated many of the results in geometric optics that the Greeks had discovered, including the law of reflection: the angle of incidence is equal to the angle of reflection. In the 13th century, such men as Roger Bacon, Robert Grosseteste, and John Pecham, relying on the work of Ibn al-Haytham (Alhazen; died c. 1040), considered numerous optical problems, including the optics of the rainbow.

It was Kepler, taking his lead from the writings of these 13th-century opticians, who set the tone for the science in the 17th century. Kepler introduced the point-by-point analysis of optical problems, tracing rays from each point on the object to a point on the image. Just as the mechanical philosophy was breaking the world into atomic parts, so Kepler approached optics by breaking organic reality into what he considered to be ultimately real units. He developed a geometric theory of lenses, providing the first mathematical account of Galileo's telescope.

Descartes sought to incorporate the phenomena of light into mechanical philosophy by demonstrating that they can be explained entirely in terms of matter and motion. Using mechanical analogies, he was able to derive mathematically many of the known properties of light, including the law of reflection and the newly discovered law of refraction.

Many of the most important contributions to optics in the 17th century were the work of Newton, especially the theory of colours. Traditional theory considered colours to be the result of the modification of white light. Descartes, for example, thought that colours were the result of the spin of the particles that constitute light. Newton upset the traditional theory of colours by demonstrating in an impressive set of experiments that white light is a mixture out of which separate beams of coloured light can be separated. He associated different degrees of refrangibility with rays of different colours, and in this manner he was able to explain the way prisms produce spectra of colours from white light.

Newton's experimental method was characterized by a quantitative approach, since he always sought measurable variables and a clear distinction between experimental findings and mechanical explanations of those findings. His second important contribution to optics dealt with the interference phenomena that came to be called "Newton's rings." Although the colours of thin films (e.g., oil on water) had been previously observed, no one had attempted to quantify the phenomena in any way. Newton observed quantitative relations between the thickness of the film and the diameters of the rings of colour, a regularity he attempted to explain by his theory of fits of easy transmission and fits of easy reflection. Notwithstanding the fact that he generally conceived of light as being particulate, Newton's theory of fits involves periodicity and vibrations of ether, the hypothetical fluid substance permeating all space.

Huygens was the second great optical thinker of the 17th century. Although he was critical of many of the details of Descartes's system, he wrote in the Cartesian tradition, seeking purely mechanical explanations of phenomena. Huygens regarded light as something of a pulse phenomenon, but he explicitly denied the periodicity of light pulses. He developed the concept of wave front, by means of which he was able to derive the laws of reflection and refraction from his pulse theory and to explain the recently discovered phenomenon of double refraction.

CHEMISTRY

Chemistry had manifold origins, coming from such diverse sources as philosophy, alchemy, metallurgy, and medicine. It emerged as a separate science only with the rise of mechanical philosophy in the 17th century. Aristotle had regarded the four elements earth, air, fire, and water as the ultimate constituents of all things. Transmutable each into the other, all four elements were believed to exist in every substance. Originating in Egypt and the Middle East, alchemy had a double aspect: on the one hand it was a practical endeavour aimed to make gold from baser substances, while on the other it was a cosmological theory based on the correspondence between man and the universe at large. Alchemy contributed to chemistry a long tradition of experience with a wide variety of substances. Paracelsus, a 16th-century Swiss natural philosopher, was a seminal figure in the history of chemistry, putting together in an almost impenetrable combination the Aristotelian theory of matter, alchemical correspondences, mystical forms of knowledge, and chemical therapy in medicine. His influence was widely felt in succeeding generations.

During the first half of the 17th century, there were few established doctrines that chemists generally accepted as a framework. As a result, there was little cumulative growth of chemical knowledge. Chemists tended to build detailed systems, "chemical philosophies," attempting to explain the entire universe in chemical terms. Most chemists accepted the traditional four elements (earth, air, fire, water) or the Paracelsian principles (salt, sulfur, mercury) or both as the bearers of real qualities in substances; they also exhibited a marked tendency toward the occult.

THE ROYAL SOCIETY OF LONDON

The Royal Society of London for Improving Natural Knowledge originated on November 28, 1660, when 12 men met after a lecture at Gresham College, London, by Christopher Wren and resolved to set up "a Colledge for the promoting of Physico-Mathematicall Experimentall Learning." Those present included the scientists Robert Boyle and Bishop John Wilkins and the courtiers Sir Robert Moray and William, 2nd Viscount Brouncker. The body set up that day was consciously new, with ambitions to become a truly national society devoted to the promotion of science. These ambitions were put into effect over the next few years, particularly through a charter of incorporation granted by Charles II in 1662 and revised in 1663.

From the outset the society aspired to combine the role of research institute with that of clearinghouse for knowledge and forum for arbitration. A key development was the establishment in 1665 of a periodical that acted as the society's mouthpiece: this was the *Philosophical Transactions*, which still flourishes today as the oldest scientific journal in continuous publication.

In the subsequent history of the society, various episodes are of particular significance. The presidency of Sir Isaac Newton from 1703 to 1727 saw this great mathematician and physicist asserting the society's dominant role in science in Britain and farther afield. Endowments from the 18th century onward made possible prizes for various aspects of science that are still awarded today—most notably the Copley Medal, which, stemming from a bequest by Sir Godfrey Copley in 1709, became the most prestigious scientific award in Britain. In the late 18th century the society played an active role in encouraging scientific exploration, particularly under its longest-serving president, Sir Joseph Banks, who earlier had accompanied James Cook on his great voyage of discovery of 1768–71. However, in general the 18th and early 19th centuries saw the society tending to rest on its laurels and become slightly amateurish. This was rectified in the 1830s by a reform program that reinvigorated the society and restored it to a prominence that it has retained ever since. In 1919 the society sent expeditions to photograph the solar eclipse of May 29 from Príncipe Island in the Gulf of Guinea and from Sobral in Brazil, verifying Albert Einstein's general theory of relativity and helping to make Einstein famous.

The Royal Society is still the leading national organization for the promotion of scientific research in Britain; it is also the oldest national scientific society in the world. Election to the Society's Fellowship is a coveted accolade for scientists; today there are approximately 1,300 fellows and 130 foreign members. Since 1967 the society has occupied premises in Carlton House Terrace, London. The society's role now includes the provision of independent advice on issues of current concern, and it also administers large sums of public money through grants aimed to support innovative research, foster international scientific cooperation, and encourage better communication between scientists and the public.

The interaction between chemistry and mechanical philosophy altered this situation by providing chemists with a shared language. The mechanical philosophy had been successfully employed in other areas; it seemed consistent with an experimental empiricism and seemed to provide a way to render chemistry respectable by translating it into the terms of the new science. Perhaps the best example of the influence of the mechanical philosophy is the work of Robert Boyle. The thrust of his work was to understand the chemical properties of matter, to provide experimental evidence for the mechanical philosophy,

and to demonstrate that all chemical properties can be explained in mechanical terms. He was an excellent laboratory chemist and developed a number of important techniques, especially colour-identification tests.

MEDICINE

The Renaissance was much more than just a reviving of interest in Greek and Roman culture; it was also a change of outlook, an eagerness for discovery, a desire to escape from the limitations of tradition and to explore new fields of thought and action. This desire was felt in the medical sciences no less than in the physical sciences. In the 16th century medical schools throughout Europe still used *The Canon of Medicine*, written 500 years earlier by Avicenna, the Persian "Prince of Physicians," as well as the writings of the Greco-Roman physician Galen, who had flourished in the 2nd and 3rd centuries CE. Galen had stressed the value of anatomy, and he had virtually founded experimental physiology. He had recognized that the arteries contain blood and not merely air, and he had showed how the heart sets the blood in motion in an ebb and flow fashion. On the other hand, he had no idea that the blood circulates. Dissection of the human body was at that time illegal, so that he was forced to base his knowledge upon the examination of monkeys, pigs, sheep, goats, and dogs. A voluminous writer who stated his views forcibly and with confidence, Galen remained for centuries the undisputed authority from whom no one dared to differ. It was perhaps natural, then, that anatomy, the knowledge of the human body, should be the first aspects of medical learning to receive attention from those who realized the need for reform.

THE ANATOMISTS

The new learning, born in Italy, grew and expanded slowly. Among the teachers of medicine in the universities there were many who clung to the past, but there were also not a few who determined to explore new lines of thought. One of these, as early as the 14th century, was Mondino dei Liucci, who taught at Bologna. Prohibitions against human dissection were slowly lifting, and Mondino performed his own dissections rather than following the customary procedure of entrusting the task to a menial. His *Anathomia*, published in 1316, was the first practical manual of anatomy. Foremost among the surgeons of the day was Guy de Chauliac, a physician to three popes at Avignon. His *Chirurgia magna* ("Great Surgery"), based on observation and experience, had a profound influence upon the progress of surgery.

It was in 1543 that Andreas Vesalius, a young Belgian professor of anatomy at the University of Padua, published *De humani corporis fabrica* ("On the Fabric of the Human Body"). Based on his own dissections, this seminal work corrected many of Galen's errors. By his scientific observations and methods, Vesalius showed that Galen could no longer be regarded as the final authority. His work at Padua was continued by Gabriel Fallopius and, later, by Hieronymus Fabricius; it was his work on the valves in the veins, *De venarum ostiolis* (1603), that suggested to his pupil William Harvey his revolutionary theory of the circulation of the blood, one of the great medical discoveries.

Surgery profited from the new outlook in anatomy, and the great reformer Ambroise Paré dominated the field in the 16th century. Paré was surgeon to four kings of France, and he has deservedly been called the father of modern surgery. In his autobiography, written after he had retired from 30 years of service as an army surgeon, Paré described

Engraving from the title page of De humani corporis fabrica, *by Belgian anatomist Andreas Vesalius, depicting a crowd observing a human dissection.* Science & Society Picture Library/Getty Images

how he had abolished the painful practice of cauterization to stop bleeding and used ligatures and dressings instead. His favourite expression, "I dressed him; God healed him," is characteristic of this humane and careful doctor.

In Britain during this period, surgery, which was performed by barber-surgeons, was becoming regulated and organized under royal charters. Companies were thus formed that eventually became the royal colleges of surgeons in Scotland and England. Physicians and surgeons united in a joint organization in Glasgow, and a college of physicians was founded in London.

The 16th-century medical scene was enlivened by the enigmatic physician and alchemist who called himself Paracelsus. Born in Switzerland, he traveled extensively throughout Europe, gaining medical skills and practicing and teaching as he went. In the tradition of Hippocrates, Paracelsus stressed the power of nature to heal, but, unlike Hippocrates, he believed also in the power of supernatural forces, and he violently attacked the medical treatments of his day. Eager for reform, he allowed his intolerance to outweigh his discretion, as when he prefaced his lectures at Basel by publicly burning the works of Avicenna and Galen. The authorities and medical men were understandably outraged. Widely famous in his time, Paracelsus remains a controversial figure to this day. Despite his turbulent career, however, he did attempt to bring a more rational approach to diagnosis and treatment, and he introduced the use of chemical drugs in place of herbal remedies.

A contemporary of Paracelsus, Girolamo Fracastoro of Italy, was a scholar cast from a very different mold. His account of the disease syphilis, entitled *Syphilis sive morbus Gallicus* (1530; "Syphilis or the French Disease"), was written in verse. Although Fracastoro called syphilis the French disease, others called it the Neapolitan disease, for it was said to have been brought to Naples from America by the sailors of Christopher Columbus. (Its origin is still questioned, in fact.) Fracastoro was interested in epidemic infection, and he offered the first scientific explanation of disease transmission. In his great work, *De contagione et contagiosis morbis* (1546), he theorized that the seeds of certain diseases are imperceptible particles transmitted by air or by contact.

THE FUTILE SEARCH FOR AN EASY SYSTEM

During the 17th century, several attempts were made to discover an easy system that would guide the practice of medicine. A substratum of superstition still remained. Richard Wiseman, surgeon to Charles II, affirmed his belief in the "royal touch" as a cure for king's evil, or scrofula, while even the learned English physician Thomas Browne stated that witches really existed. There was, however, a general desire to discard the past and adopt new ideas.

The view of René Descartes that the human body is a machine and that it functions mechanically had its repercussions in medical thought. One group adopting this explanation called themselves the iatrophysicists; another school, preferring to view life as a series of chemical processes, were called iatrochemists. Santorio Santorio, working at Padua, was an early exponent of the iatrophysical view and a pioneer investigator of metabolism. He was especially concerned with the measurement of what he called "insensible perspiration," described in his book *De Statica Medicina* (1614; "On Medical Measurement"). Another Italian, who developed the idea still further, was Giovanni Alfonso Borelli, a professor of mathematics at Pisa, who gave his attention to the mechanics and

Sir Christopher Wren, one of the founders of the Royal Society.
© Photos.com/Thinkstock

statics of the body and to the physical laws that govern its movements.

The iatrochemical school was founded at Brussels by Jan Baptista van Helmont, whose writings are tinged with the mysticism of the alchemist. A more logical and intelligible view of iatrochemistry was advanced by Franciscus Sylvius, at Leiden, and in England a leading exponent of the same school was Thomas Willis, who is better known for his description of the brain in his *Cerebri Anatome, cui accessit Nervorum descriptio et usus* (1664; "Anatomy of the Brain, with a Description of the Nerves and Their Function"), published in 1664 and illustrated by the designer Christopher Wren.

It soon became apparent that no easy road to medical knowledge and practice was to be found along these channels and that the best method was the age-old system of straightforward clinical observation. The rewards due to those who adhered to these values were illustrated by William Harvey, whose explanation of the circulation of blood was the supreme achievement in medicine in the 17th century.

HARVEY AND THE EXPERIMENTAL METHOD

Born in Folkestone, England, Harvey studied at Cambridge and then spent several years at Padua, where he came under the influence of Fabricius. He established a successful medical practice in London and, by precise observation and scrupulous reasoning, developed his theory of circulation. In 1628 he published his classic book *Exercitatio Anatomica de Motu Cordis et Sanguinis in Animalibus* (*Anatomical Exercise on the Motion of the Heart and Blood in Animals*), often called *De Motu Cordis*.

That the book aroused controversy is not surprising. There were still many who adhered to the teaching of

Galen that the blood follows an ebb-and-flow movement in the blood vessels. Harvey's work was the result of many careful experiments, but few of his critics took the trouble to repeat the experiments, simply arguing in favour of the older view. His second great book, *Exercitationes de Generatione Animalium* ("Exercises on the Generation of Animals"), published in 1651, laid the foundation of modern embryology.

Harvey's discovery of the circulation of the blood was a landmark of medical progress; the new experimental method by which the results were secured was as noteworthy as the work itself. Following the method described by the philosopher Francis Bacon, he drew the truth from experience and not from authority.

There was one gap in Harvey's argument: he was obliged to assume the existence of capillary vessels that conveyed the blood from the arteries to the veins. This gap persisted until the work of Marcello Malpighi of Bologna (who was born in 1628, the year of publication of *De Motu Cordis*). With a primitive microscope, Malpighi saw a network of tiny blood vessels in the lung of a frog, and with that he supplied the missing link in the chain of evidence proving the circulation of the blood.

MICROSCOPY

The magnifying power of segments of glass spheres was known to the Assyrians before the time of Christ; during the 2nd century CE, Ptolemy wrote a treatise on optics in which he discussed the phenomena of magnification and refraction as related to such lenses and to glass spheres filled with water. Despite this knowledge, however, glass lenses were not used extensively until around 1300, when some anonymous person invented spectacles for the improvement of vision. This invention aroused curiosity concerning the property of lenses to magnify, and in the 16th century several papers were written about such devices. Then, near the end of the 16th century, it was discovered that if certain lenses are mounted together in a tube, they would form what physicists now call a Galilean telescope when viewed through one end, and a compound microscope when viewed through the other. When, in the early 1600s, Galileo used this instrument to examine the stars and planets, he was able to record such new discoveries as the rings of Saturn and the four satellites of Jupiter.

Although Galileo is often credited with making the first biological observations with the microscope, he did not make any further contributions to its development. Following technological improvements in the instrument and the development of a more liberal attitude toward scientific research, a new generation of microscopists emerged who were to have a profound effect on biology. Among these were Marcello Malpighi, Robert Hooke, and Antonie van Leeuwenhoek.

MALPIGHI'S ANIMAL AND PLANT STUDIES

Malpighi, an Italian biologist and physician, conducted extensive studies in animal anatomy and histology (the microscopic study of the structure, composition, and function of tissues). He was the first to describe the inner (malpighian) layer of the skin, the papillae of the tongue, the outer part (cortex) of the cerebral area of the brain, and the red blood cells. He wrote a detailed monograph on the silkworm; a further major contribution was a description of the development of the chick, beginning with the 24-hour stage. In addition to these and other animal studies, Malpighi made detailed investigations in plant anatomy. He systematically described the various parts of plants, such as bark, stem, roots, and seeds, and discussed such processes as germination and gall formation; he may even have suspected that plants were made up of cells, a concept that had not yet been introduced.

Many of Malpighi's drawings of plant anatomy remained unintelligible to botanists until the structures were rediscovered in the 19th century. Although Malpighi was not a technical innovator, he does exemplify the functioning of the educated 17th-century mind, which, together with curiosity and patience, resulted in many advances in biology.

THE DISCOVERY OF CELLS

Of the great Renaissance microscopists, Robert Hooke was perhaps the most intellectually preeminent. As curator of instruments at the Royal Society of London, he was in touch with all new scientific developments and exhibited interest in such disparate subjects as flying and the construction of clocks. In 1665 Hooke published his *Micrographia*, which was primarily a review of a series of observations that he had made while following the development and improvement of the microscope. Among the items Hooke described in detail were the structure of feathers, the stinger of a bee, the radula, or "tongue," of mollusks, and the foot of the fly.

It is Hooke who coined the word "cell." In a drawing of the microscopic structure of cork, he showed walls surrounding empty spaces and refers to these structures as cells. He described similar structures in the tissue of other trees and plants and discerned that in some tissues the cells were filled with a liquid while in others they were empty. He therefore supposed that the function of the cells was to transport substances through the plant.

THE DISCOVERY OF "ANIMALCULES"

Antonie van Leeuwenhoek, a Dutchman who spent most of his life in Delft, sold cloth for a living. As a young man, however, he became interested in grinding lenses, which he mounted in gold, silver, or copper plates. Indeed, he became so obsessed with the idea of making perfect lenses that he neglected his business and was ridiculed by his family and neighbours. Using single lenses rather than compound ones (a system of two or more), Leeuwenhoek achieved magnifications from 40 to 270 diameters, a remarkable feat for hand-ground lenses. Among his most conspicuous observations was the discovery in 1675 of the existence in stagnant water and prepared infusions of many protozoans, which he called animalcules. He observed the connections between the arteries and veins; gave particularly fine accounts of the microscopic structure of muscle, the lens of the eye, the teeth, and other structures; and recognized bacteria of different shapes, postulating that they must be on the order of 25 times as small as the red blood cell. Because this is the approximate size of bacteria, it indicates that his observations were correct. Leeuwenhoek's fame was consolidated when he confirmed the observations of a student that male seminal fluid contains spermatozoa. Furthermore, he discovered spermatozoa in other animals as well as in the female tract following copulation; the latter destroyed the idea held by others that the entire future development of an animal is centred in the egg, and that sperm merely induce a "vapour," which penetrates the womb and effects fertilization. Although this theory of preformation, as it is called, continued to survive for some time longer, Leeuwenhoek initiated its eventual demise.

Leeuwenhoek's animalcules raised some disquieting thoughts in the minds of his contemporaries. The theory

An early microscope (right) *purportedly used by Robert Hooke. Shown with the microscope is a copy of the mechanism used to illuminate subjects being observed by the microscopist.* Science & Society Picture Library/Getty Images

of spontaneous generation, held by the ancient world and passed down unquestioned, was now being criticized. Christiaan Huygens, a scientific friend of Leeuwenhoek, hypothesized that these little animals might be small enough to float in the air and, on reaching water, reproduce themselves. At this time, however, criticism of spontaneous generation went no further.

MICROSCOPY AND THE SCIENTIFIC METHOD

Although the work of any of the early microscopists seems to lack a definite objective, it should be remembered that these men embodied the concept that observation and experiment were of prime importance, that mere hypothetical, philosophical speculations were not sufficient. It is remarkable that so few men, working as individuals totally isolated from each other, should have recorded so many observations of such fundamental importance. The great significance of their work was that it revealed, for the first time, a world in which living organisms display an almost incredible complexity.

TECHNOLOGY AND RENAISSANCE SCIENCE

Technology performed a service for the scientific revolution by providing it with instruments that greatly enhanced its powers. The use of the telescope by Galileo to observe the moons of Jupiter is a dramatic example of this service, but the telescope was only one of many tools and instruments that proved valuable in navigation, mapmaking, and laboratory experiments. More significant were the services of the new sciences to technology, and the most important of these was the theoretical preparation for the invention of the steam engine. The researches of a number of scientists, especially those of Robert Boyle of England with atmospheric pressure, of Otto von Guericke of Germany with a vacuum, and of the French Huguenot Denis Papin with pressure vessels, helped to equip practical technologists with the theoretical basis of steam power. Distressingly little is known about the manner in which this knowledge was assimilated by pioneers such as Thomas Savery, but it is inconceivable that they could have been ignorant of it.

The most important technological advance of all, because it underlay progress in so many other fields, was the development of printing, with movable metal type, about the mid-15th century in Germany. Johannes Gutenberg is usually called its inventor, but in fact many people and many steps were involved. Block printing on wood came to the West from China between 1250 and 1350, papermaking came from China by way of the Arabs to 12th-century Spain, whereas the Flemish technique of oil painting was the origin of the new printers' ink. Three men of Mainz—Gutenberg and his contemporaries Johann Fust and Peter Schöffer—seem to have taken the final steps, casting metal type and locking it into a wooden press. The invention spread like the wind, reaching Italy by 1467, Hungary and Poland in the 1470s, and Scandinavia by 1483. By 1500 the presses of Europe had produced some six million books. Without the printing press it is impossible to conceive that the the rise of a new science, which was a cooperative effort of an international community, would have occurred at all. In short, the development of printing amounted to a communications revolution of the order of the invention of writing; and, like that prehistoric discovery, it transformed the conditions of life.

The growing flood of information put heavy strains upon old institutions and practices. It was no longer sufficient to publish scientific results in an expensive book that few could buy; information had to be spread widely and rapidly. Nor could the isolated genius, like Newton, comprehend a world in which new information was being produced faster than any single person could assimilate it. Natural philosophers had to be sure of their data, and to that end they required independent and critical confirmation of their discoveries. New means were created to accomplish these ends. Scientific societies sprang up, beginning in Italy in the early years of the 17th century and culminating in the two great national scientific societies that mark the zenith of the scientific revolution: the Royal Society of London, created by royal charter in 1662, and the Académie des Sciences of Paris, formed in 1666. In these societies and others like them all over the world, natural philosophers could gather to examine, discuss, and criticize new discoveries and old theories. To provide a firm basis for these discussions, societies began to publish scientific papers. The Royal Society's *Philosophical Transactions*, which began as a private venture of its secretary, was the first such professional scientific journal. It was soon copied by the French academy's *Mémoires*, which won equal importance and prestige. The old practice of hiding new discoveries in private jargon, obscure language, or even anagrams gradually gave way to the ideal of universal comprehensibility. New canons of reporting were devised so that experiments and discoveries could be reproduced by others. This required new precision in language and a willingness to share experimental or observational methods. The failure of others to reproduce results cast serious doubts upon the original reports. Thus were created the tools for a massive assault on nature's secrets.

Astronomers

The Renaissance is justly famous for its astronomers, for they, by daring to place the Sun, and not Earth, at the centre of the cosmos, fired the opening shot in the scientific revolution. Only a century passed between the publication of Nicolaus Copernicus's great book *De revolutionibus orbium coelestium libri vi* ("Six Books Concerning the Revolutions of the Heavenly Orbs") and the death of Galileo. But the work of these great men, along with that of Tycho Brahe and Johannes Kepler, was to bear consequences greater than those of any other intellectual event in the history of humankind.

NICOLAUS COPERNICUS

(b. Feb. 19, 1473, Toruń, Poland—d. May 24, 1543, Frauenburg, East Prussia [now Frombork, Poland])

Nicolaus Copernicus (Polish Mikołaj Kopernik) was a Polish astronomer who proposed that the planets have the Sun as the fixed point to which their motions are to be referred; that Earth is a planet that, besides orbiting the Sun annually, also turns once daily on its own axis; and that very slow, long-term changes in the direction of this axis account for the precession of the equinoxes. This representation of the heavens is usually called the heliocentric,

Statue of Nicolaus Copernicus in Krakow, Poland. The figure of Copernicus is holding a globe showing the known planets revolving around the Sun. Henryk T. Kaiser/Photolibrary/Getty Images

or "Sun-centred," system—derived from the Greek *helios*, meaning "Sun." Copernicus's theory had important consequences for later thinkers of the scientific revolution, including such major figures as Galileo, Kepler, Descartes, and Newton.

Copernicus probably hit upon his main idea sometime between 1508 and 1514, and during those years he wrote a manuscript usually called the *Commentariolus* ("Little Commentary"). However, the book that contains the final version of his theory, *De revolutionibus orbium coelestium libri vi* ("Six Books Concerning the Revolutions of the Heavenly Orbs"), did not appear in print until 1543, the year of his death.

EARLY LIFE AND EDUCATION

Certain facts about Copernicus's early life are well established, although a biography written by his ardent disciple Georg Joachim Rheticus (1514–74) is unfortunately lost. According to a later horoscope, Nicolaus Copernicus was born in Toruń, a city in north-central Poland on the Vistula River south of the major Baltic seaport of Gdańsk. His father, Nicolaus, was a well-to-do merchant, and his mother, Barbara Watzenrode, also came from a leading merchant family. Nicolaus was the youngest of four children. After his father's death, sometime between 1483 and 1485, his mother's brother Lucas Watzenrode (1447–1512) took his nephew under his protection. Watzenrode, soon to be bishop of the chapter of Varmia (Warmia), saw to young Nicolaus's education and his future career as a church canon.

Between 1491 and about 1494 Copernicus studied liberal arts—including astronomy and astrology—at the University of Cracow (Kraków). Like many students of his time, however, he left before completing his degree, resuming his studies in Italy at the University of Bologna, where his uncle had obtained a doctorate in canon law in 1473. The Bologna period (1496–1500) was short but significant. For a time Copernicus lived in the same house as the principal astronomer at the university, Domenico Maria de Novara (1454–1504). Novara had the responsibility of issuing annual astrological prognostications for the city, forecasts that included all social groups but gave special attention to the fate of the Italian princes and their enemies. Copernicus, as is known from Rheticus, was "assistant and witness" to some of Novara's observations, and his involvement with the production of the annual forecasts means that he was intimately familiar with the practice of astrology.

Novara also probably introduced Copernicus to two important books that framed his future problematic as a student of the heavens: *Epitoma in Almagestum Ptolemaei* ("Epitome of Ptolemy's Almagest") by Johann Müller (also known as *Regiomontanus*, 1436–76) and *Disputationes adversus astrologianm divinatricenm* ("Disputations against Divinatory Astrology") by Giovanni Pico della Mirandola (1463–94). The first provided a summary of the foundations of Ptolemy's astronomy, with *Regiomontanus*'s corrections and critical expansions of certain important planetary models that might have been suggestive to Copernicus of directions leading to the heliocentric hypothesis. Pico's *Disputationes* offered a devastating skeptical attack on the foundations of astrology that reverberated into the 17th century. Among Pico's criticisms was the charge that, because astronomers disagreed about the order of the planets, astrologers could not be certain about the strengths of the powers issuing from the planets.

In 1500 Copernicus spoke before an interested audience in Rome on mathematical subjects, but the exact content of his lectures is unknown. In 1501 he stayed briefly in Frauenburg but soon returned to Italy to continue his studies, this time at the University of Padua, where he pursued medical studies between 1501 and 1503. At this time medicine was closely allied with astrology, as the stars were thought to influence the body's dispositions. Thus, Copernicus's astrological experience at Bologna was better training for medicine than one might imagine today. Copernicus later painted a self-portrait; it is likely that he acquired the necessary artistic skills while in Padua, since there was a flourishing community of painters there and in nearby Venice.

In May 1503 Copernicus finally received a doctorate—like his uncle, in canon law—but from an Italian university where he had not studied: the University of Ferrara. When he returned to Poland, Bishop Watzenrode arranged a sinecure for him: an in absentia teaching post, or scholastry, at Wrocław. Copernicus's actual duties at the bishopric palace, however, were largely administrative and medical. As a church canon, he collected rents from church-owned lands; secured military defenses; oversaw chapter finances; managed the bakery, brewery, and mills; and cared for the medical needs of the other canons and his uncle. Copernicus's astronomical work took place in his spare time, apart from these other obligations.

COPERNICUS'S ASTRONOMICAL WORK

In Copernicus's period, astrology and astronomy were considered subdivisions of a common subject called the "science of the stars," whose main aim was to provide a description of the arrangement of the heavens as well as the theoretical tools and tables of motions that would permit accurate construction of horoscopes and annual prognostications. At this time the terms astrologer, astronomer, and mathematician were virtually interchangeable; they generally denoted anyone who studied the heavens using mathematical techniques.

Pico claimed that astrology ought to be condemned because its practitioners were in disagreement about everything, from the divisions of the zodiac to the minutest observations to the order of the planets. A second long-standing disagreement, not mentioned by Pico, concerned the status of the planetary models. From antiquity, astronomical modeling was governed by the premise that the planets move with uniform angular motion on fixed radii at a constant distance from their centres of motion. Two types of models derived from this premise. The first, represented by that of Aristotle, held that the planets are carried around the centre of the universe embedded in unchangeable, material, invisible spheres at fixed distances. Since all planets have the same centre of motion, the universe is made of nested, concentric spheres with no gaps between them.

As a predictive model, this account was of limited value. Among other things, it had the distinct disadvantage that it could not account for variations in the apparent brightness of the planets since the distances from the centre were always the same. A second tradition, deriving from Claudius Ptolemy, solved this problem by postulating three mechanisms: uniformly revolving, off-centre circles called eccentrics; epicycles, little circles whose centres moved uniformly on the circumference of circles of larger radius (deferents); and equants. The equant, however, broke with the main assumption of ancient astronomy because it separated the condition of uniform motion from that of constant distance from the centre. A planet viewed from the centre c of its orbit would appear to move sometimes faster, sometimes slower. As seen from Earth, removed a distance e from c, the planet would also appear to move nonuniformly. Only from the equant, an imaginary point at distance 2e from Earth, would the planet appear to move uniformly. A planet-bearing sphere revolving around an equant point will wobble; situate one sphere within another, and the two will collide, disrupting the heavenly order.

In the 13th century a group of Persian astronomers at Marāgheh had discovered that, by combining two uniformly revolving epicycles to generate an oscillating point that would account for variations in distance, they could devise a model that produced the equalized motion without referring to an equant point. The Marāgheh work was written in Arabic, which Copernicus did not read. However, he learned to do the Marāgheh "trick," either independently or through a still-unknown intermediary link. This insight was the starting point for his attempt to resolve the conflict raised by wobbling physical spheres.

Copernicus might have continued this work by considering each planet independently, as did Ptolemy in the *Almagest*, without any attempt to bring all the models together into a coordinated arrangement. However, he was also disturbed by Pico's charge that astronomers could not agree on the actual order of the planets. The difficulty focused on the locations of Venus and Mercury. There was general agreement that the Moon and Sun encircled the motionless Earth and that Mars, Jupiter, and Saturn were situated beyond the Sun in that order. However, Ptolemy placed Venus closest to the Sun and Mercury to the Moon, while others claimed that Mercury and Venus were beyond the Sun. In the *Commentariolus*, Copernicus postulated that, if the Sun is assumed to be at rest and if Earth is assumed to be in motion, then the remaining planets fall into an orderly relationship whereby their sidereal periods increase from the Sun as follows: Mercury (88 days), Venus (225 days), Earth (1 year), Mars (1.9 years), Jupiter (12 years), and Saturn (30 years).

This theory did resolve the disagreement about the ordering of the planets, but, in turn, it raised new problems. To accept the theory's premises, one had to abandon much of Aristotelian natural philosophy and develop a new explanation for why heavy bodies fall to a moving Earth. It was also necessary to explain how a transient body like Earth, filled with meteorological phenomena, pestilence, and wars, could be part of a perfect and imperishable heaven.

Any of these considerations alone could account for Copernicus's delay in publishing his work. (He remarked in the preface to *De revolutionibus* that he had chosen to withhold publication not for merely the nine years recommended by the Roman poet Horace but for 36 years, four times that period.) And, when a description of the main elements of the heliocentric hypothesis was first published, in the *Narratio prima* (1540 and 1541, "First Narration"), it was not under Copernicus's own name but under that of the 25-year-old Georg Rheticus. Rheticus, a Lutheran from the University of Wittenberg, Germany, stayed with Copernicus at Frauenburg for about two and a half years, between 1539 and 1542. The *Narratio prima* was, in effect, a joint production of Copernicus and Rheticus, something of a "trial balloon" for the main work.

Both Rheticus and Copernicus knew that they could not definitively rule out all possible alternatives to the heliocentric theory. But they could underline what Copernicus's theory provided that others could not: a singular method for ordering the planets and for calculating the relative distances of the planets from the Sun. Rheticus compared this new universe to a well-tuned musical instrument and to the interlocking wheel-mechanisms of a clock. In the preface to *De revolutionibus*, Copernicus used an image from Horace's *Ars poetica* ("Art of Poetry"). The theories of his predecessors, he wrote, were like a human figure in which the arms, legs, and head were put together in the form of a disorderly monster. His own representation of the universe, in contrast, was an orderly whole in which a displacement of any part would result in a disruption of the whole. In effect, a new criterion of scientific adequacy was advanced together with the new theory of the universe.

PUBLICATION OF *DE REVOLUTIONIBUS*

The presentation of Copernicus's theory in its final form is inseparable from the conflicted history of its publication. When Rheticus left Frauenburg to return to his teaching duties at Wittenberg, he took the manuscript with him in order to arrange for its publication at Nürnberg, the leading centre of printing in Germany. He chose the top printer in the city, Johann Petreius, who had published a number of ancient and modern astrological works during the 1530s. It was not uncommon for authors to participate directly in the printing of their manuscripts, sometimes even living in the printer's home. However, Rheticus was unable to remain and supervise. He turned the manuscript over to Andreas Osiander (1498–1552), a theologian experienced in shepherding mathematical books through production as well as a leading political figure in the city and an ardent follower of Luther (although he was eventually expelled from the Lutheran church). In earlier communication with Copernicus, Osiander had urged him to present his ideas as purely hypothetical, and he now introduced certain changes without the permission of either Rheticus or Copernicus. Osiander added an unsigned "letter to the reader" directly after the title page, which maintained that the hypotheses contained within made no pretense to truth and that, in any case, astronomy was incapable of finding the causes of heavenly phenomena. Rheticus's rage was so great that he crossed out the letter with a great red X in the copies sent to him. In addition, the title of the work was changed from the manuscript's "On the Revolutions of the Orbs of the World" to "Six Books Concerning the Revolutions of the Heavenly Orbs"—a change that appeared to mitigate the book's claim to describe the real universe.

Legend has it that a copy of *De revolutionibus* was placed in Copernicus's hands a few days after he lost consciousness from a stroke. He awoke long enough to realize that he was holding his great book and then expired, publishing as he perished. The legend has some credibility, although it also has the beatific air of a saint's life.

TYCHO BRAHE

(b. Dec. 14, 1546, Knudstrup, Scania, Denmark—d. Oct. 24, 1601, Prague)

Tycho Brahe was a Danish astronomer whose work in developing astronomical instruments and in measuring and fixing the positions of stars paved the way for future discoveries. His observations—the most accurate possible before the invention of the telescope—included a comprehensive study of the solar system and accurate positions of more than 777 fixed stars.

YOUTH AND EDUCATION

Tycho's father was a privy councillor and later governor of the castle of Helsingborg, which controls the main waterway to the Baltic Sea. His wealthy and childless uncle abducted Tycho at a very early age and, after the initial parental shock was overcome, raised him at his castle in Tostrup, Scania, also financing the youth's education, which began with the study of law at the University of Copenhagen in 1559–62.

Several important natural events turned Tycho from law to astronomy. The first was the total eclipse of the Sun predicted for Aug. 21, 1560. Such a prediction seemed audacious and marvelous to a 14-year-old student, but when Tycho witnessed its realization he saw and believed—the spark was lit—and, as his many later references testify, he never forgot the event. His subsequent student life was divided between his daytime lectures on jurisprudence, in response to the wishes of his uncle, and his nighttime vigil of the stars. The professor of mathematics helped him with the only printed astronomical book available, the *Almagest* of Ptolemy, the astronomer of antiquity who described the geocentric conception of the cosmos. Other teachers helped him to construct small globes, on which star positions could be plotted, and compasses and cross-staffs, with which he could estimate the angular separation of stars.

In 1562 Tycho's uncle sent him to the University of Leipzig, where he studied until 1565. Another significant event in Tycho's life occurred in August 1563, when he made his first recorded observation, a conjunction, or overlapping, of Jupiter and Saturn. Almost immediately he found that the existing almanacs and ephemerides, which record stellar and planetary positions, were grossly inaccurate. The Copernican tables were several days off in predicting this event. In his youthful enthusiasm Tycho decided to devote his life to the accumulation of accurate observations of the heavens, in order to correct the existing tables.

Between 1565 and 1570 (or 1572?) he traveled widely throughout Europe, studying at Wittenberg, Rostock, Basel, and Augsburg and acquiring mathematical and astronomical instruments, including a huge quadrant. Inheriting the estates of his father and of his uncle Jørgen, Tycho then settled in Scania in 1571(?) and constructed a small observatory on property owned by a relative. Here occurred the third and most important astronomical event in Tycho's life. On November 11, 1572, he suddenly saw a "new star," brighter than Venus and where no star was supposed to be, in the constellation Cassiopeia. He carefully observed the new star and showed that it lay beyond the Moon and therefore was in the realm of the fixed stars. To the world at the time, this was a disquieting discovery, because the intellectual community protected itself against the uncertainties of the future by confidence in the Aristotelian doctrine of inner and continuous harmony of the whole world. This harmony was ruled by the stars, which were regarded as perfect and unchanging. The news that a star could change as dramatically as that described by Tycho, together with the reports of the Copernican theory that the Sun, not Earth, was the centre of the universe, shook confidence in the immutable laws of antiquity and suggested that the chaos and imperfections of Earth were reflected in the heavens. Tycho's discovery of the new star in Cassiopeia in 1572 and his publication of his observations of it in *De nova stella* in 1573 marked his transformation from a Danish dilettante to an astronomer with a European reputation.

By marrying a peasant's daughter, named Kirstine, in 1573, Tycho—as a nobleman's son—scandalized most of his contemporaries. He seldom mentioned her in his extensive correspondence (which still exists), and it is probable that he was interested mainly in a companion who would superintend his household without being involved in court functions and intrigues. Tycho and Kirstine had eight children, six of whom survived him.

Portrait of Danish astronomer Tycho Brahe, known primarily for his mapping of fixed stars. Leemage/Universal Images Group/ Getty Images

MATURE CAREER

The new star in the constellation Cassiopeia had caused Tycho to rededicate himself to astronomy; one immediate decision was to establish a large observatory for regular observations of celestial events. His plan to establish this observatory in Germany prompted King Frederick II to keep him in Denmark by granting him title in 1576 to the island of Ven (formerly Hven), in the middle of The Sound and about halfway between Copenhagen and Helsingør, together with financial support for the observatory and laboratory buildings. Tycho called the observatory Uraniborg, after Urania, the Muse of astronomy. Surrounded by scholars and visited by learned travelers from all over Europe, Tycho and his assistants collected observations and substantially corrected nearly every known astronomical record.

Tycho was an artist as well as a scientist and craftsman, and everything he undertook or surrounded himself with had to be innovative and beautiful. He established a printing shop to produce and bind his manuscripts in his own way, he imported Augsburg craftsmen to construct the finest astronomical instruments, he induced Italian and Dutch artists and architects to design and decorate his observatory, and he invented a pressure system to provide the then uncommon convenience of sanitary lavatory facilities. Uraniborg fulfilled the hopes of Tycho's king and friend, Frederick II, that it would become the centre of astronomical study and discovery in northern Europe.

But Frederick died in 1588, and under his son, Christian IV, Tycho's influence dwindled; most of his income was stopped, partly because of the increasing needs of the state for money. Spoiled by Frederick, however, Tycho had become both unreasonably demanding of more money and less inclined to carry out the civic duties required by his income from state lands.

At odds with the three great powers—king, church, and nobility—Tycho left Ven in 1597, and, after short stays at Rostock and at Wandsbek, near Hamburg, he settled in Prague in 1599 under the patronage of Emperor Rudolf II, who also in later years supported the astronomer Johannes Kepler.

The major portion of Tycho's lifework—making and recording accurate astronomical observations—had already been done at Uraniborg. To his earlier observations, particularly his proof that the nova of 1572 was a star, he added a comprehensive study of the solar system and his proof that the orbit of the comet of 1577 lay beyond the Moon. He proposed a modified Copernican system in which the planets revolved around the Sun, which in turn moved around the stationary Earth. What Tycho accomplished, using only his simple instruments and practical talents, remains an outstanding accomplishment of the Renaissance.

Tycho attempted to continue his observations at Prague with the few instruments he had salvaged from Uraniborg, but the spirit was not there, and he died in 1601, leaving all his observational data to Kepler, his pupil and assistant in the final years. With these data Kepler laid the groundwork for the work of Sir Isaac Newton.

JOHANNES KEPLER

(b. Dec. 27, 1571, Weil der Stadt, Württemberg [Germany]—d. Nov. 15, 1630, Regensburg)

Johannes Kepler was a German astronomer who discovered three major laws of planetary motion, conventionally designated as follows: (1) the planets move in elliptical orbits with the Sun at one focus; (2) the time

Portrait of Johannes Kepler, the German astronomer who discovered three laws of planetary motion. Imagno/Hulton Archive/Getty Images

necessary to traverse any arc of a planetary orbit is proportional to the area of the sector between the central body and that arc (the "area law"); and (3) there is an exact relationship between the squares of the planets' periodic times and the cubes of the radii of their orbits (the "harmonic law").

Kepler himself did not call these discoveries "laws," as would become customary after Isaac Newton derived them from a new and quite different set of general physical principles. He regarded them as celestial harmonies that reflected God's design for the universe. Kepler's discoveries turned Nicolaus Copernicus's Sun-centred system into a dynamic universe, with the Sun actively pushing the planets around in noncircular orbits. And it was Kepler's notion of a physical astronomy that fixed a new problematic for other important 17th-century world-system builders, the most famous of whom was Newton.

KEPLER'S SOCIAL WORLD

Kepler came from a very modest family in a small German town and was one of the beneficiaries of a ducal scholarship for poor boys; it made possible his attendance at the Lutheran Stift, or seminary, at the University of Tübingen, where he began his university studies in 1589. It was expected that the boys who graduated from these schools would go on to become schoolteachers, ministers, or state functionaries. Kepler had planned to become a theologian.

His life did not work out quite as he expected. As he sometimes remarked, Divine Providence guided him to the study of the stars, while he retained a profound sense that his vocation was a religious one. As he later wrote, "I am satisfied...to guard the gates of the temple in which Copernicus makes sacrifices at the high altar." It helped also that, at Tübingen, the professor of mathematics was Michael

Maestlin (1550–1631), one of the most talented astronomers in Germany. Maestlin had once been a Lutheran pastor; he was also, privately, one of the few adherents of the Copernican theory in the late 16th century, although very cautious about expressing his views in print.

Maestlin lent Kepler his own heavily annotated copy of Copernicus's 1543 book, *De revolutionibus orbium coelestium libri vi* ("Six Books Concerning the Revolutions of the Heavenly Orbs"). Kepler quickly grasped the main ideas in Copernicus's work and was tutored in its complex details by Maestlin. He sensed intuitively that Copernicus had hit upon an account of the universe that contained the mark of divine planning—literally a revelation. Early in the 1590s, while still a student, Kepler would make it his mission to demonstrate rigorously what Copernicus had only guessed to be the case. And he did so in an explicitly religious and philosophical vocabulary. Kepler's God was a dynamic, creative being whose presence in the world was symbolized by the Sun's body as the source of a dynamic force that continually moved the planets. The natural world was like a mirror that precisely reflected and embodied these divine ideas. Inspired by Platonic notions of innate ideas in the soul, Kepler believed that the human mind was ideally created to understand the world's structure.

ASTRONOMICAL WORK

The ideas that Kepler would pursue for the rest of his life were already present in his first work, *Mysterium cosmographicum* (1596; "Cosmographic Mystery"). In 1595, while teaching a class at a small Lutheran school in Graz, Austria, Kepler experienced a moment of illumination. It struck him suddenly that the spacing among the six Copernican planets might be explained by circumscribing

and inscribing each orbit with one of the five regular polyhedrons. Since Kepler knew Euclid's proof that there can
be five and only five such mathematical objects made up
of congruent faces, he decided that such self-sufficiency
must betoken a perfect idea. If now the ratios of the mean
orbital distances agreed with the ratios obtained from circumscribing and inscribing the polyhedrons, then, Kepler
felt confidently, he would have discovered the architecture
of the universe. Remarkably, Kepler did find agreement
within 5 percent, with the exception of Jupiter, at which,
he said, "no one will wonder, considering such a great distance." He wrote to Maestlin at once: "I wanted to become
a theologian; for a long time I was restless. Now, however,
behold how through my effort God is being celebrated in
astronomy."

Had Kepler's investigation ended with the establishment of this architectonic principle, he might have
continued to search for other sorts of harmonies; but
his work would not have broken with the ancient Greek
notion of uniform circular planetary motion. Kepler's
God, however, was not only orderly but also active. In
place of the tradition that individual incorporeal souls
push the planets and instead of Copernicus's passive, rest-
ing Sun, Kepler posited the hypothesis that a single force
from the Sun accounts for the increasingly long periods
of motion as the planetary distances increase. Kepler did
not yet have an exact mathematical description for this
relation, but he intuited a connection. A few years later
he acquired William Gilbert's groundbreaking book *De
Magnete, Magneticisque Corporibus, et de Magno Magnete
Tellure* (1600; "On the Magnet, Magnetic Bodies, and the
Great Magnet, the Earth"), and he immediately adopted
Gilbert's theory that Earth is a magnet. From this Kepler
generalized to the view that the universe is a system of
magnetic bodies in which, with corresponding like poles

134   DE MOTIB. STELLÆ MARTIS

CAP.
XXIV.

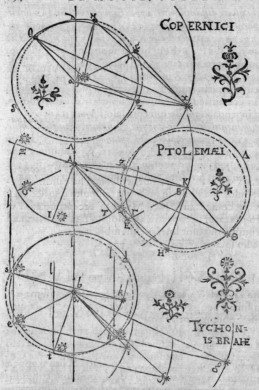

COPERNICI

PTOLEMÆI

TYCHO-
NIS BRAHE

ſtrabitur (ut prius) iisdem plane numeris, lineis & angulis, has lineas præter opinionem eſſe inæquales, ac propterea Martem non in circulo Γ Δ verſari, cujus ſit centrum in K puncto æqualitatis motus, ſed in ZEHΘ circulo, cujus centrum a K verſus B vergat, propemodum in linea KB. quæ ſit parallelos lineæ ex A TERRA per perigæum SOLIS ductu.

Vergit igitur apogæum epicycli in perigæum SOLIS. Et quia epicyclus propter omnimodam æquipollentiam, ut jam dictu, ponendus eſt æqualis circuitui Solis, & ZK parallelos

ipſi ΞA, & EK ipſi OA, & HK ipſi IA, & ΘK ipſi TA: igitur etiam ipſas ΞA, OA, IA, TA, inæquales eſſe veriſimile eſt: & punctum medii loci SOLIS (BRAHEANA notione centrum epicycli SOLIS) per circuitum a puncto æqualitatis diſtare inæqualiter. Quod obiter interjeci. nihil .n. facit ad præſentem demonſtrationem, niſi quod eam extendit amplius.

In forma TYCHONICA ſit A TERRA, & ex ea ſcribatur SOLIS concentricus CD, qui putetur eſſe deferens SYSTEMA *Planetarum;* cum ſit A punctum æqualitatis motus concentrici SOLIS. Erit itaque SOL ipſe in alio eccentrico circulo. Sit ejus centrum ab A verſus partes B. Sit autem AL regula lineæ apſidum MARTIS, ut linea apſidum circulatione & transpoſitione ſui eccentrici ſemper maneat parallelos ipſi AL. Sint autem lineæ medii motus SOLIS ad noſtra quatuor momenta AH, AT, AE, AS: & ex A ejiciantur lineæ viſionum MARTIS, prout ſupra deſcriptæ ſunt, in hunc vel illum zodiaci gradum vergere. Et quia ponitur MARS omnibus quatuor vicibus eodem

repelling and unlike poles attracting, the rotating Sun sweeps the planets around. The solar force, attenuating inversely with distance in the planes of the orbits, was the major physical principle that guided Kepler's struggle to construct a better orbital theory for Mars.

But there was something more: the standard of empirical precision that Kepler held for himself was unprecedented for his time. The great Danish astronomer Tycho Brahe (1546–1601) had set himself the task of amassing a completely new set of planetary observations—a reform of the foundations of practical astronomy. In 1600 Tycho invited Kepler to join his court at Castle Benátky near Prague. When Tycho died suddenly in 1601, Kepler quickly succeeded him as imperial mathematician to Holy Roman emperor Rudolf II.

The relatively great intellectual freedom possible at Rudolf's court was now augmented by Kepler's unexpected inheritance of a critical resource: Tycho's observations. In his lifetime Tycho had been stingy in sharing his observations. After his death, although there was a political struggle with Tycho's heirs, Kepler was ultimately able to work with data accurate to within 2′ of arc. Without data of such precision to back up his solar hypothesis, Kepler would have been unable to discover his "first law" (1605), that Mars moves in an elliptical orbit. At one point, for example, as he tried to balance the demand for the correct heliocentric distances predicted by his physical model with a circular orbit, an error of 6′ or 8′ appeared in the octants (assuming a circle divided into eight equal parts). Kepler exclaimed, "Because these 8′ could not be ignored, they alone have led to a total reformation of astronomy."

During the creative burst of the early Prague period (1601–05) when Kepler won his "war on Mars" (he did not publish his discoveries until 1609 in the *Astronomia Nova* [*New Astronomy*]), he also wrote important treatises on

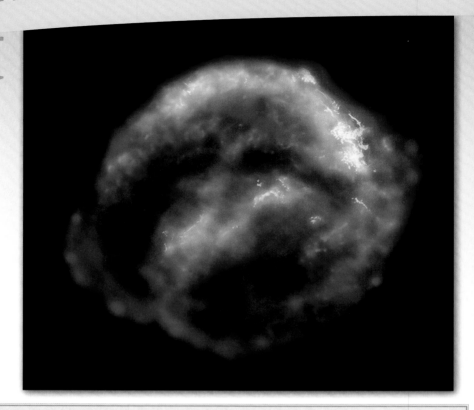

Composite image of Kepler's Nova, or Kepler's Supernova, taken by the Chandra X-ray Observatory. NASA, ESA, R. Sankrit and W. Blair, Johns Hopkins University

the nature of light and on the sudden appearance of a new star (1606; *De Stella Nova*, "On the New Star"). Kepler first noticed the star—now known to have been a supernova—in October 1604, not long after a conjunction of Jupiter and Saturn in 1603. The astrological importance of the long-anticipated conjunction (such configurations take place every 20 years) was heightened by the unexpected appearance of the supernova. Typically, Kepler used the occasion both to render practical predictions (e.g., the collapse of Islam and the return of Christ) and to speculate theoretically about the universe—for example, that the star was not the result of chance combinations of atoms and that stars are not suns.

After Galileo built a telescope in 1609 and announced hitherto-unknown objects in the heavens (e.g., moons revolving around Jupiter) and imperfections of the lunar surface, he sent Kepler his account in *Siderius Nuncius* (1610; *The Sidereal Messenger*). Kepler responded with three important treatises. The first was his *Dissertatio cum Nuncio Sidereo* (1610; "Conversation with the Sidereal Messenger"), in which, among other things, he speculated that the distances of the newly discovered Jovian moons might agree with the ratios of the rhombic dodecahedron, triacontahedron, and cube. The second was a theoretical work on the optics of the telescope, *Dioptrice* (1611; "Dioptrics"), including a description of a new type of telescope using two convex lenses. The third was based upon his own observations of Jupiter, made between Aug. 30 and Sept. 9, 1610, and published as *Narratio de Jovis Satellitibus* (1611; "Narration Concerning the Jovian Satellites"). These works provided strong support for Galileo's discoveries, and Galileo, who had never been especially generous to Kepler, wrote to him, "I thank you because you were the first one, and practically the only one, to have complete faith in my assertions."

In 1611 Kepler's life took a turn for the worse. His wife, Barbara, became ill, and his three children contracted smallpox; one of his sons died. Emperor Rudolf soon abdicated his throne. Although Kepler hoped to return to an academic post at Tübingen, there was resistance from the theology faculty; Kepler's irenic theological views and his friendships with Calvinists and Catholics were characteristic of his independence in all matters, and in this case it did not help his cause. Meanwhile, Kepler was appointed to the position (created for him) of district mathematician in Linz. He continued to hold the position of imperial mathematician under the new emperor, Matthias, although he was physically removed from the court in Prague. Kepler stayed in Linz until 1626, during which time creative productions continued amid personal troubles—the death of his wife and his exclusion from the Lutheran communion. Although he was married again in 1613 (to Susanna Reuttinger), five of his seven children from that marriage died in childhood. After the Counter-Reformation came in 1625, Catholic authorities temporarily removed his library and ordered his children to attend mass.

The Linz authorities had anticipated that Kepler would use most of his time to work on and complete the astronomical tables begun by Tycho. But the work was tedious, and Kepler continued his search for the world harmonies that had inspired him since his youth. In 1619 his *Harmonice Mundi* (*Harmonies of the World*) brought together more than two decades of investigations into the archetypal principles of the world: geometrical, musical, metaphysical, astrological, astronomical, and those principles pertaining to the soul.

Finally, Kepler published the first textbook of Copernican astronomy, *Epitome Astronomiae Copernicanae* (1618–21; *Epitome of Copernican Astronomy*). The title mimicked Maestlin's traditional-style textbook, but the content could not have been more different. The *Epitome* began with the elements of astronomy but then gathered together all the arguments for Copernicus's theory and added to them Kepler's harmonics and new rules of planetary motion. This work would prove to be the most important theoretical resource for the Copernicans in the 17th century. Galileo and Descartes were probably influenced by it.

The last decade of Kepler's life was filled with personal anguish. His mother fell victim to a charge of witchcraft that resulted in a protracted battle with her accusers, lasting from 1615 until her exoneration in 1621; she died a few months later. Kepler used all means at his disposal to save his mother's life and honour, but the travels, legal briefs, and maneuvers that this support required seriously disrupted his work. In 1627 Kepler found a new patron in the imperial general Albrecht von Wallenstein. Wallenstein sent Kepler to Sagan in Silesia and supported the construction of a printing press for him. In return Wallenstein expected horoscopes from Kepler—and he accurately predicted "horrible disorders" for March 1634, close to the actual date of Wallenstein's murder on Feb. 25, 1634. Kepler was less successful in his ever-continuing struggle to collect monies owed him. In August 1630 Wallenstein lost his position as commander in chief; in October Kepler left for Regensburg in hopes of collecting interest on some Austrian bonds. But soon after arriving he became seriously ill with fever, and on Nov. 15 he died. His grave was swept away in the Thirty Years' War, but the epitaph that he composed for himself survived:

> *I used to measure the heavens,*
> *now I shall measure the shadows of the earth.*
> *Although my soul was from heaven,*
> *the shadow of my body lies here.*

GALILEO

(b. Feb. 15, 1564, Pisa [Italy]—d. Jan. 8, 1642, Arcetri, near Florence)

Galileo Galilei was an Italian natural philosopher, astronomer, and mathematician who made fundamental contributions to the sciences of motion, astronomy, and strength of materials and to the development of the scientific method. His formulation of (circular) inertia, the law

REFRACTING AND REFLECTING TELESCOPES

The telescope, the primary astronomical instrument, is said to have been invented about 1608 by the Dutch optician Hans Lippershey, but Galileo is credited with having developed it for astronomical observation immediately after, in 1609. The largest of his instruments was only about 120 cm (47 inches) long and had a diameter of 5 cm (2 inches), but Galileo used them to explore such celestial phenomena as the valleys and mountains of the Moon, the phases of Venus, and the four largest satellites of Jupiter.

Galileo's telescopes were of the refracting type. The term "refraction" refers to the bending of light when it passes from one medium to another of different density—e.g., from air to the glass lens of a telescope. In a refractor the first lens through which light from a celestial object passes is called the objective lens. Galileo's objective lens was convex; it gathered parallel rays

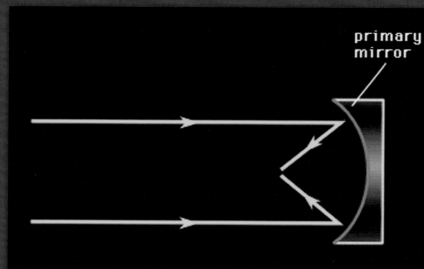

primary mirror

©1994 Encyclopaedia Britannica, Inc.

Concave mirror.

of light from the heavens and directed them toward a point, called the focus, at which they would converge. The distance between the objective lens and the focus is known as the focal length, and the focal length essentially determines the length of the telescope. It should be mentioned that an image seen at the focus would be inverted. Galileo solved this problem by placing a second lens, the eyepiece, inside the focal length. The eyepiece was concave and refracted the gathering light onto a parallel path to the observer's eye, which saw a magnified, upright image.

The reflecting telescope was developed in 1668 by Isaac Newton. Instead of refracting light through an objective lens, it contained a concave spherical primary mirror at the far end of the tube that reflected the light back to a focus near the upper end. Obviously, if an observer put his eye at the upper end of the telescope to view the reflected image, his head would block the light from reaching the mirror. Newton solved this problem by placing a small flat secondary mirror at an angle of 45° inside the focal length and thereby brought the focus to the side of the telescope tube, where his eyepiece was located.

Reflecting telescopes have two well-known advantages over refractors. They are not subject to chromatic aberration because reflected light does not disperse according to wavelength, as happens with refraction. Also, the tube of a reflector is shorter than that of a refractor of the same diameter. The Newtonian reflector is still popular among amateur telescope makers.

An alternative reflector design was conceived in 1663 by Newton's contemporary, the Scottish astronomer James Gregory. Gregory proposed using a parabolic primary mirror to reflect the light and then using a concave secondary mirror to reflect the light back through a small hole in the primary mirror to a focus located behind the primary. In 1672 Laurent Cassegrain of France invented another type of reflector. The Cassegrainian telescope employed a small convex secondary mirror to reflect the light back through a hole in the primary mirror.

of falling bodies, and parabolic trajectories marked the beginning of a fundamental change in the study of motion. His insistence that the book of nature was written in the language of mathematics changed natural philosophy from a verbal, qualitative account to a mathematical one in which experimentation became a recognized method for discovering the facts of nature. Finally, his discoveries with the telescope revolutionized astronomy and paved the way for the acceptance of the Copernican heliocentric system. However, his advocacy of the Copernican system eventually resulted in an Inquisition process being brought against him, and he was sentenced to house arrest near Florence for the last nine years of his life.

EARLY LIFE AND CAREER

Galileo was born the oldest son of Vincenzo Galilei, a musician who made important contributions to the theory and practice of music and who may have performed some experiments with Galileo in 1588–89 on the relationship between pitch and the tension of strings. In the early 1570s the family moved to Florence, where the Galilei family had lived for generations. In his middle teens Galileo attended the monastery school at Vallombrosa, near Florence, and then in 1581 he matriculated at the University of Pisa, where he was to study medicine. However, he became enamoured with mathematics and decided to make the mathematical subjects and philosophy his profession, against the protests of his father. Galileo then began to prepare himself to teach Aristotelian philosophy and mathematics, and several of his lectures have survived. In 1585 Galileo left the university without having obtained a degree, and for several years he gave private lessons in the mathematical subjects in Florence and Siena. During this period he designed a new form of hydrostatic balance for weighing small quantities and wrote a short treatise, La *bilancetta* ("The Little Balance"), that circulated in manuscript form. He also began his studies on motion, which he pursued steadily for the next two decades.

In 1588 Galileo applied for the chair of mathematics at the University of Bologna but was unsuccessful. His reputation was, however, increasing, and later that year he was asked to deliver two lectures to the Florentine Academy, a prestigious literary group, on the arrangement of the world in Dante's *Inferno*. He also found some ingenious theorems on centres of gravity (again, circulated in manuscript) that brought him recognition among mathematicians and the patronage of Guidobaldo del Monte (1545–1607), a nobleman and author of several important works on mechanics. As a result, he obtained the chair of mathematics at the University of Pisa in 1589. There, according to his first biographer, Vincenzo Viviani (1622–1703), Galileo demonstrated, by dropping bodies of different weights from the top of the famous Leaning Tower, that the speed of fall of a heavy object is not proportional to its weight, as Aristotle had claimed. The manuscript tract *De motu* (*On Motion*), finished during this period, shows that Galileo was abandoning Aristotelian notions about motion and was instead taking an Archimedean approach to the problem. But his attacks on Aristotle made him unpopular with his colleagues, and in 1592 his contract was not renewed. His patrons, however, secured him the chair of mathematics at the University of Padua, where he taught from 1592 until 1610.

Although Galileo's salary was considerably higher there, his responsibilities as the head of the family (his father had died in 1591) meant that he was chronically pressed for money. His university salary could not cover all his expenses, and he therefore took in well-to-do boarding students whom he tutored privately in such subjects as fortification. He also sold a proportional compass, or sector, of his own devising, made by an artisan whom he employed in his house. Perhaps because of these financial problems, he did not marry, but he did have an arrangement with a Venetian woman, Marina Gamba, who bore him two daughters and a son. In the midst of his busy life he continued his research on motion, and by 1609 he had determined that the distance fallen by a body is proportional to the square of the elapsed time (the law of falling bodies) and that the trajectory of a projectile is a parabola, both conclusions that contradicted Aristotelian physics.

TELESCOPIC DISCOVERIES

At this point, however, Galileo's career took a dramatic turn. In the spring of 1609 he heard that in the Netherlands an instrument had been invented that showed distant things as though they were nearby. By trial and error, he quickly figured out the secret of the invention and made his own three-powered spyglass from lenses for sale in spectacle makers' shops. Others had done the same, but what set Galileo apart was that he quickly figured out how to improve the instrument, taught himself the art of lens grinding, and produced increasingly powerful telescopes. In August of that year he presented an eight-powered instrument to the Venetian Senate (Padua was in the Venetian Republic). He was rewarded with life tenure and a doubling of his salary. Galileo was now one of the highest-paid professors at the university.

In the fall of 1609 Galileo began observing the heavens with instruments that magnified up to 20 times. In December he drew the Moon's phases as seen through the telescope, showing that the Moon's surface is not smooth, as had been thought, but is rough and uneven. In January 1610 he discovered four moons revolving around Jupiter.

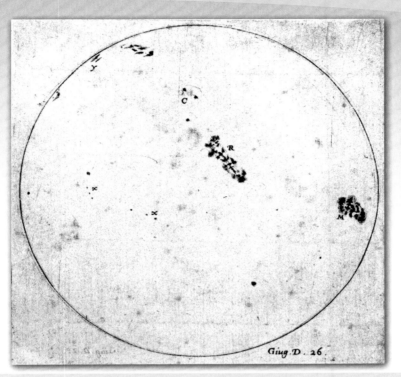

Illustration from Galileo's Istoria e dimostrazioni intorno alle macchie solari e loro accidenti *("History and Demonstrations Concerning Sunspots and Their Properties," or "Letters on Sunspots"),* 1613. © Photos.com/Thinkstock

He also found that the telescope showed many more stars than are visible with the naked eye. These discoveries were earthshaking, and Galileo quickly produced a little book, *Sidereus Nuncius* (*The Sidereal Messenger*), in which he described them. He dedicated the book to Cosimo II de Medici (1590–1621), the grand duke of his native Tuscany, whom he had tutored in mathematics for several summers, and he named the moons of Jupiter after the Medici family: the Sidera Medicea, or "Medicean Stars." Galileo was rewarded with an appointment as mathematician and philosopher of the grand duke of Tuscany, and in the fall of 1610 he returned in triumph to his native land.

Galileo was now a courtier and lived the life of a gentleman. Before he left Padua he had discovered the puzzling appearance of Saturn, later to be shown as caused by a ring surrounding it, and in Florence he discovered that Venus goes through phases just as the Moon does. Although these discoveries did not prove that Earth is a planet orbiting the Sun, they undermined Aristotelian cosmology: the absolute difference between the corrupt earthly region and the perfect and unchanging heavens was proved wrong by the mountainous surface of the Moon, the moons of Jupiter showed that there had to be more than one centre of motion in the universe, and the phases of Venus showed that it (and, by implication, Mercury) revolves around the Sun. As a result, Galileo was confirmed in his belief, which he had probably held for decades but which had not been central to his studies, that the Sun is the centre of the universe and that Earth is a planet, as Copernicus had argued. Galileo's conversion to Copernicanism would be a key turning point in the scientific revolution.

GALILEO'S COPERNICANISM

Galileo's increasingly overt Copernicanism began to cause trouble for him. In 1613 he wrote a letter to his student Benedetto Castelli (1577–1644) in Pisa about the problem of squaring the Copernican theory with certain biblical passages. Inaccurate copies of this letter were sent by Galileo's enemies to the Inquisition in Rome, and he had to retrieve the letter and send an accurate copy. Several Dominican fathers in Florence lodged complaints against Galileo in Rome, and Galileo went to Rome to defend the Copernican cause and his good name. Before leaving, he finished an expanded version of the letter to

Castelli, now addressed to the grand duke's mother and good friend of Galileo, the dowager Christina. In his *Letter to the Grand Duchess Christina*, Galileo discussed the problem of interpreting biblical passages with regard to scientific discoveries but, except for one example, did not actually interpret the Bible. That task had been reserved for approved theologians in the wake of the Council of Trent (1545–63) and the beginning of the Catholic Counter-Reformation.

But the tide in Rome was turning against the Copernican theory, and in 1615, when the cleric Paolo Antonio Foscarini (c. 1565–1616) published a book arguing that the Copernican theory did not conflict with scripture, Inquisition consultants examined the question and pronounced the Copernican theory heretical. Foscarini's book was banned, as were some more technical and non-theological works, such as Johannes Kepler's *Epitome of Copernican Astronomy*. Copernicus's own 1543 book, *De revolutionibus orbium coelestium libri vi* ("Six Books Concerning the Revolutions of the Heavenly Orbs"), was suspended until corrected. Galileo was not mentioned directly in the decree, but he was admonished by Robert Cardinal Bellarmine (1542–1621) not to "hold or defend" the Copernican theory. An improperly prepared document placed in the Inquisition files at this time states that Galileo was admonished "not to hold, teach, or defend" the Copernican theory "in any way whatever, either orally or in writing."

Galileo was thus effectively muzzled on the Copernican issue. Only slowly did he recover from this setback. Through a student, he entered a controversy about the nature of comets occasioned by the appearance of three comets in 1618. After several exchanges, mainly with Orazio Grassi (1583–1654), a professor of mathematics at the Collegio Romano, he finally entered the argument

under his own name. *Il saggiatore* (*The Assayer*), published in 1623, was a brilliant polemic on physical reality and an exposition of the new scientific method. Galileo here discussed the method of the newly emerging science, arguing:

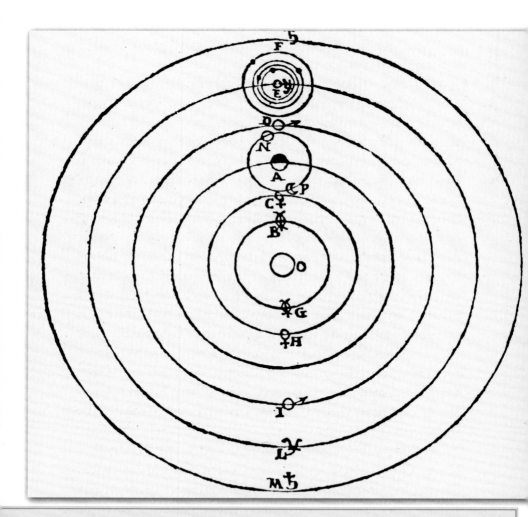

Illustration of the Copernican system of the universe from Galileo's Dialogo sopra i due massimi sistemi del mondo, tolemaico e copernicano (Dialogue Concerning the Two Chief World Systems, Ptolemaic & Copernican), *1632.*
© Photos.com/Thinkstock

Philosophy is written in this grand book, the universe, which stands continually open to our gaze. But the book cannot be understood unless one first learns to comprehend the language and read the letters in which it is composed. It is written in the language of mathematics, and its characters are triangles, circles, and other geometric figures without which it is humanly impossible to understand a single word of it.

He also drew a distinction between the properties of external objects and the sensations they cause in us—i.e., the distinction between primary and secondary qualities. Publication of *Il saggiatore* came at an auspicious moment, for Maffeo Cardinal Barberini (1568–1644), a friend, admirer, and patron of Galileo for a decade, was named Pope Urban VIII as the book was going to press. Galileo's friends quickly arranged to have it dedicated to the new pope. In 1624 Galileo went to Rome and had six interviews with Urban VIII. Galileo told the pope about his theory of the tides (developed earlier), which he put forward as proof of the annual and diurnal motions of Earth. The pope gave Galileo permission to write a book about theories of the universe but warned him to treat the Copernican theory only hypothetically.

The book, *Dialogo sopra i due massimi sistemi del mondo, tolemaico e copernicano* (*Dialogue Concerning the Two Chief World Systems, Ptolemaic & Copernican*), was finished in 1630, and Galileo sent it to the Roman censor. Because of an outbreak of the plague, communications between Florence and Rome were interrupted, and Galileo asked for the censoring to be done instead in Florence. The Roman censor had a number of serious criticisms of the book and forwarded these to his colleagues in Florence. After writing a preface in which he professed that what followed was written hypothetically, Galileo had little trouble getting the book through the Florentine censors, and it appeared in Florence in 1632.

GALILEO AND THE INQUISITION

In the *Dialogue*'s witty conversation between Salviati (representing Galileo), Sagredo (the intelligent layman), and Simplicio (the dyed-in-the-wool Aristotelian), Galileo gathered together all the arguments (mostly based on his own telescopic discoveries) for the Copernican theory and against the traditional geocentric cosmology. As opposed to Aristotle's, Galileo's approach to cosmology is fundamentally spatial and geometric: Earth's axis retains its orientation in space as Earth circles the Sun, and bodies not under a force retain their velocity (although this inertia is ultimately circular). But in giving Simplicio the final word, that God could have made the universe any way he wanted to and still made it appear to us the way it does, he put Pope Urban VIII's favourite argument in the mouth of the person who had been ridiculed throughout the dialogue.

Reaction against the book was swift. A special commission, convened by the pope to examine the book, found that Galileo had not really treated the Copernican theory hypothetically and recommended that a case be brought against him by the Inquisition. Galileo was summoned to Rome in 1633. During his first appearance before the Inquisition, he was confronted with the 1616 edict recording that he was forbidden to discuss the Copernican theory. In his defense Galileo produced a letter from Cardinal Bellarmine, by then dead, stating that he was admonished only not to hold or defend the theory. The case was at somewhat of an impasse, and, in what can only be called a plea bargain, Galileo confessed to having overstated his case. He was pronounced to be

Galileo (right) *stands before papal magistrates of the Inquisition. Galileo ran afoul of Pope Urban VIII for ideas presented in the astronomer's* Dialogue *and was accused of heresy.* DEA Picture Library/Getty Images

vehemently suspect of heresy and was condemned to life imprisonment and was made to abjure formally. There is no evidence that at this time he whispered, "Eppur si muove" ("And yet it moves"). It should be noted that Galileo was never in a dungeon or tortured; during the Inquisition process he stayed mostly at the house of the Tuscan ambassador to the Vatican and for a short time in a comfortable apartment in the Inquisition building. After the process he spent six months at the palace of Ascanio Piccolomini (c. 1590–1671), the archbishop of Siena and a friend and patron, and then moved into a villa near Arcetri, in the hills above Florence. He spent the rest of his life there. Galileo's daughter Sister Maria Celeste, who was in a nearby nunnery, was a great comfort to her father until her untimely death in 1634.

Galileo was then 70 years old. Yet he kept working. In Siena he had begun a new book on the sciences of motion and strength of materials. There he wrote up his unpublished studies that had been interrupted by his interest in the telescope in 1609 and pursued intermittently since. The book was spirited out of Italy and published in Leiden, Netherlands, in 1638 under the title *Discorsi e dimostrazioni matematiche intorno a due nuove scienze attenenti alla meccanica* (*Dialogues Concerning Two New Sciences*). Galileo here treated for the first time the bending and breaking of beams and summarized his mathematical and experimental investigations of motion, including the law of falling bodies and the parabolic path of projectiles as a result of the mixing of two motions, constant speed and uniform acceleration. By then Galileo had become blind, and he spent his time working with a young student, Vincenzo Viviani, who was with him when he died.

Natural Philosophers

Before terms such as "science," "physics," and "chemistry" began to be used with their modern meanings, those who observed the material world and contemplated the laws that governed it were known as "natural philosophers." Natural philosophy frequently shaded over into astronomy on one side and physiology on the other, as the objects of these disciplines, too, were understood to behave according to laws that could be discerned by observation. For this reason it is difficult to define René Descartes, Isaac Newton, Christiaan Huygens, and Robert Boyle strictly as physicists, chemists, or any other kinds of scientist. By turns they were any one of these and also all of them — true Renaissance men.

RENÉ DESCARTES

(b. March 31, 1596, La Haye, Touraine, France — d. Feb. 11, 1650, Stockholm, Sweden)

René Descartes was a French mathematician, scientist, and philosopher. Because he was one of the first to abandon scholastic Aristotelianism, because he formulated the first modern version of mind-body dualism, from which stems the mind-body problem, and because he promoted the development of a new science grounded in observation and experiment, he has been called the father of modern philosophy. Applying an original system of methodical doubt, he dismissed apparent knowledge derived from authority, the senses, and reason and erected new epistemic foundations on the basis of the intuition that, when he is thinking, he exists; this he expressed in the dictum "I think, therefore I am" (best known in its Latin formulation, "Cogito, ergo sum," though originally written in French, "Je pense, donc je suis").

EARLY LIFE AND EDUCATION

Although Descartes's birthplace was in Touraine, his family connections lay south, across the Creuse River in Poitou, where his father, Joachim, owned farms and houses in Châtellerault and Poitiers. Because Joachim was a councillor in the Parlement of Brittany in Rennes, Descartes inherited a modest rank of nobility. Descartes's mother died when he was one year old. His father remarried in Rennes, leaving him in La Haye to be raised first by his maternal grandmother and then by his great-uncle in Châtellerault. Although the Descartes family was Roman Catholic, the Poitou region was controlled by the Protestant Huguenots.

In 1606 Descartes was sent to the Jesuit college at La Flèche, where young men were trained for careers in military engineering, the judiciary, and government

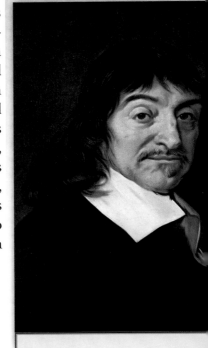

French philosopher and scientist René Descartes, whose work melded psychology, philosophy, medicine, and physiology. Image Hulton Archive/Getty Images

administration. In 1614 he went to Poitiers, where he took a law degree in 1616. Descartes's father probably expected him to enter Parlement, but the minimum age for doing so was 27, and Descartes was only 20. In 1618 he went to Breda in the Netherlands, where he spent 15 months as an informal student of mathematics and military architecture in the peacetime army of the Protestant stadholder, Prince Maurice (ruled 1585–1625).

Descartes spent the period 1619 to 1628 traveling in northern and southern Europe. While in Bohemia in 1619, he invented analytic geometry, a method of solving geometric problems algebraically and algebraic problems geometrically. He also devised a universal method of deductive reasoning, based on mathematics, that is applicable to all the sciences. He later formulated this method in *Discourse on Method* (1637) and *Rules for the Direction of the Mind* (written by 1628 but not published until 1701).

In 1622 Descartes moved to Paris. There he gambled, rode, fenced, and went to the court, concerts, and the theatre. Among his friends were the mathematician Claude Mydorge (1585–1647) and Father Marin Mersenne (1588–1648), a man of universal learning who corresponded with hundreds of scholars, writers, mathematicians, and scientists and who became Descartes's main contact with the larger intellectual world. During this time Descartes acquired a considerable reputation long before he published anything.

At a talk in 1628, Descartes denied the alchemist Chandoux's claim that probabilities are as good as certainties in science and demonstrated his own method for attaining certainty. The Cardinal Pierre de Bérulle (1575–1629)—who had founded the Oratorian teaching congregation in 1611 as a rival to the Jesuits—was present at the talk. Within weeks Descartes left for the Netherlands, which was Protestant, and—taking great precautions to conceal his address—did not return to France for 16 years. Some scholars claim that Descartes adopted Bérulle as director of his conscience, but this is unlikely, given Descartes's background and beliefs (he came from a Huguenot province, he was not a Catholic enthusiast, he had been accused of being a Rosicrucian, and he advocated religious tolerance and championed the use of reason).

RESIDENCE IN THE NETHERLANDS

The Netherlands was a haven of tolerance, where Descartes could be an original, independent thinker without fear of being burned at the stake—as was the Italian philosopher Lucilio Vanini (1585–1619) for proposing natural explanations of miracles—or being drafted into the armies then prosecuting the Catholic Counter-Reformation. In France, by contrast, religious intolerance was mounting. In 1624 the French Parlement passed a decree forbidding criticism of Aristotle on pain of death. Although Mersenne and the philosopher Pierre Gassendi (1592–1655) did publish attacks on Aristotle without suffering persecution (they were, after all, Catholic priests), those judged to be heretics continued to be burned, and laymen lacked church protection.

In 1629 Descartes went to the university at Franeker, where he stayed with a Catholic family and wrote the first draft of his *Meditations*. He matriculated at the University of Leiden in 1630. In 1635 Descartes's daughter Francine was born to Helena Jans and was baptized in the Reformed Church in Deventer. Although Francine is typically referred to by commentators as Descartes's "illegitimate" daughter, her baptism is recorded in a register for legitimate births. Her death of scarlet fever at the age of five was the greatest sorrow of Descartes's life.

THE WORLD, THE DISCOURSE ON METHOD, AND THE MEDITATIONS

In 1633, just as he was about to publish *The World* (1664), Descartes learned that the Italian astronomer Galileo Galilei (1564–1642) had been condemned in Rome for publishing the view that Earth revolves around the Sun. Because this Copernican position was central to his cosmology and physics, Descartes suppressed *The World*, hoping that eventually the church would retract its condemnation.

Descartes's *Discourse on Method* (1637) is one of the first important modern philosophical works not written in Latin. Descartes said that he wrote in French so that all who had good sense, including women, could read his work and learn to think for themselves. He believed that everyone could tell true from false by the natural light of reason. In three essays accompanying the *Discourse*, he illustrated his method for utilizing reason in the search for truth in the sciences: in *Dioptrics* he derived the law of refraction, in *Meteorology* he explained the rainbow, and in *Geometry* he gave an exposition of his analytic geometry.

In 1641 Descartes published the *Meditations on First Philosophy, in Which Is Proved the Existence of God and the Immortality of the Soul*. Written in Latin and dedicated to the Jesuit professors at the Sorbonne in Paris, the work included critical responses by several eminent thinkers—collected by Mersenne from the Jansenist philosopher and theologian Antoine Arnauld (1612–94), the English philosopher Thomas Hobbes (1588–1679), and the Epicurean atomist Pierre Gassendi (1592–1655)—as well as Descartes's replies.

The *Meditations* is characterized by Descartes's use of methodic doubt, a systematic procedure of rejecting as though false all types of belief in which one has ever been, or could ever be, deceived. He considered the possibility that an "evil genius" with extraordinary powers has deceived him to such an extent that all his beliefs are false. But it is not possible, Descartes contended, that all his beliefs are false, for if he has false beliefs, he is thinking, and if he is thinking, then he exists. Therefore, his belief that he exists cannot be false, as long as he is thinking. This line of argument is summarized in the formula "Cogito, ergo sum" ("I think, therefore I am").

On the basis of clear and distinct innate ideas, Descartes then establishes that each mind is a mental substance and each body a part of one material substance. The mind or soul is immortal, because it is unextended and cannot be broken into parts, as can extended bodies. Descartes also advances a proof for the existence of God. He begins with the proposition that he has an innate idea of God as a perfect being and then concludes that God necessarily exists, because, if he did not, he would not be perfect.

The inherent circularity of Descartes's reasoning was exposed by Arnauld, whose objection has come to be known as the Cartesian Circle. According to Descartes, God's existence is established by the fact that Descartes has a clear and distinct idea of God; but the truth of Descartes's clear and distinct ideas are guaranteed by the fact that God exists and is not a deceiver. Thus, in order to show that God exists, Descartes must assume that God exists.

PHYSICS, PHYSIOLOGY, AND MORALS

Descartes then spent the rest of his life working in mechanics, medicine, and morals. Mechanics is the basis of his physiology and medicine, which in turn is the basis of his moral psychology. Descartes believed that all material bodies, including the human body, are machines that operate by mechanical principles. In his physiological studies, he dissected animal bodies to show how their parts move. He argued that, because animals have no souls, they do not think or feel; thus, vivisection, which Descartes practiced, is permitted. He also described the circulation of the blood but came to the erroneous conclusion that heat in the heart expands the blood, causing its expulsion into the veins. Descartes's *L'Homme, et un traité de la formation du foetus* (*Man, and a Treatise on the Formation of the Foetus*) was published in 1664.

In 1644 Descartes published *Principles of Philosophy*, a compilation of his physics and metaphysics. According to Descartes, a human being is a union of mind and body, two radically dissimilar substances that interact in the pineal gland. He reasoned that the pineal gland must be the uniting point because it is the only nondouble organ in the brain, and double reports, as from two eyes, must have one place to merge. He argued that each action on a person's sense organs causes subtle matter to move through tubular nerves to the pineal gland, causing it to vibrate distinctively. These vibrations give rise to emotions and passions and also cause the body to act. Bodily action is thus the final outcome of a reflex arc that begins with external stimuli—as, for example, when a soldier sees the enemy, feels fear, and flees. The mind cannot change bodily reactions directly—for example, it cannot will the body to fight—but by altering mental attitudes, it can change the pineal vibrations from those that cause fear and fleeing to those that cause courage and fighting.

Descartes argued further that human beings can be conditioned by experience to have specific emotional responses. Descartes himself, for example, had been conditioned to be attracted to cross-eyed women because he had loved a cross-eyed playmate as a child. When he remembered this fact, however, he was able to rid himself of his passion. This insight is the basis of Descartes's defense of free will and of the mind's ability to control the body. Despite such arguments, in his *Passions of the Soul* (1649), which he dedicated to Queen Christina of Sweden (reigned 1644–54), Descartes holds that most bodily actions are determined by external material causes.

FINAL YEARS

In 1644, 1647, and 1648, after 16 years in the Netherlands, Descartes returned to France for brief visits on financial business and to oversee the translation into French of the *Principles*, the *Meditations*, and the *Objections and Replies*. During his final stay in Paris in 1648, the French nobility revolted against the crown in a series of wars known as the Fronde. Descartes left precipitously on Aug. 17, 1648, only days before the death of his old friend Mersenne.

Hector Pierre Chanut, a French resident in Sweden and later ambassador, helped to procure a pension for Descartes from Louis XIV, though it was never paid. Later, Chanut engineered an invitation for Descartes to the court of Queen Christina, who by the close of the Thirty Years' War (1618–48) had become one of the most important and powerful monarchs in Europe. Descartes went reluctantly, arriving early in October 1649.

In Sweden—where, Descartes said, in winter men's thoughts freeze like the water—the 22-year-old Christina perversely made the 53-year-old Descartes rise before 5:00 AM to give her philosophy lessons, even though she knew of his habit of lying in bed until 11 o'clock in the morning. While delivering the statutes for a Swedish Academy of Arts and Sciences to the queen at 5:00 AM on Feb. 1, 1650, he caught a chill, and he soon developed pneumonia and died. Many pious last words have been attributed to him, but the most trustworthy report is that of his German valet, who said that Descartes was in a coma and died without saying anything at all.

ISAAC NEWTON

(b. Dec. 25, 1642 [Jan. 4, 1643, New Style], Woolsthorpe, Lincolnshire, England—d. March 20 [March 31], 1727, London)

Isaac Newton was an English physicist and mathematician who was the culminating figure of the scientific revolution of the 17th century. In optics, his discovery of the composition of white light integrated the phenomena of colours into the science of light and laid the foundation for modern physical optics. In mechanics, his three laws of motion, the basic principles of modern physics, resulted in the formulation of the law of universal gravitation. In mathematics, he was the original discoverer of the infinitesimal calculus. Newton's *Philosophiae Naturalis Principia Mathematica* (1687; *Mathematical Principles of Natural Philosophy*) was one of the most important single works in the history of modern science.

FORMATIVE INFLUENCES

A tiny and weak baby, Newton was not expected to survive his first day of life, much less 84 years. Deprived of a father before birth, he soon lost his mother when she remarried and her husband, the well-to-do minister Barnabas Smith, left young Isaac with his grandmother. For nine years, Isaac was effectively separated from his mother, and his pronounced psychotic tendencies have been ascribed to this traumatic event.

Sir Isaac Newton, portrait by John Vanderbank, c. 1725; in the collection of the Royal Astronomical Society, London. © Photos.com/Thinkstock

After his mother was widowed again, she determined that Newton should manage her now considerable property, but he could not bring himself to concentrate on rural affairs—set to watch the cattle, he would curl up under a tree with a book. Fortunately, the mistake was recognized, and Newton was sent to the grammar school in Grantham to prepare for the university.

EARLY WORK ON MOTION

When Newton arrived in Cambridge in 1661, the scientific revolution was well advanced. Yet the universities of Europe, including Cambridge, continued to be the strongholds of outmoded Aristotelianism, which rested on a geocentric view of the universe.

Newton began his higher education by immersing himself in Aristotle's work. However, on his own, without formal guidance, he had sought out the new philosophy and the new mathematics and made them his own, but he had confined the progress of his studies to his notebooks. Then, in 1665, the plague closed the university, and for most of the following two years he was forced to stay at his home. During the plague years he examined the elements of circular motion and, applying his analysis to the Moon and the planets, derived the inverse square relation that the radially directed force acting on a planet decreases with the square of its distance from the Sun—which was later crucial to the law of universal gravitation. The world heard nothing of this discovery.

About 1679, Newton began to ascribe puzzling phenomena—chemical affinities, the generation of heat in chemical reactions, surface tension in fluids, capillary action, and the cohesion of bodies—to attractions and repulsions between particles of matter. Newton originally applied the idea of attractions and repulsions solely to the range of terrestrial phenomena mentioned above. But late in 1679, another application was suggested in a letter from Robert Hooke, who was seeking to renew correspondence. Hooke mentioned his analysis of planetary motion. Newton bluntly refused to correspond but, nevertheless, mentioned an experiment to demonstrate the rotation of Earth: let a body be dropped from a tower; because the tangential velocity at the top of the tower is greater than that at the foot, the body should fall slightly to the east. He sketched the path of fall as part of a spiral ending at the centre of Earth. This was a mistake, as Hooke pointed out; according to Hooke's theory of planetary motion, the path should be elliptical, so that if Earth were split and separated to allow the body to fall, it would rise again to its original location. Newton corrected Hooke's figure using the assumption that gravity is constant. Hooke then countered by replying that, although Newton's figure was correct for constant gravity, his own assumption was that gravity decreases as the square of the distance. Several years later, this letter became the basis for Hooke's charge of plagiarism. He was mistaken in the charge. His knowledge of the inverse square relation rested only on intuitive grounds. Moreover, unknown to him, Newton had so derived the relation more than ten years earlier.

THE *PRINCIPIA*

Nearly five years later, in August 1684, Newton was visited by the British astronomer Edmond Halley, who was also troubled by the problem of orbital dynamics. Upon learning that Newton had solved the problem, he extracted Newton's promise to send the demonstration. Three months later he received a short tract entitled *De Motu* ("On Motion"). Already Newton was at work improving and expanding it. In two and a half years, the tract *De Motu* grew into *Philosophiae Naturalis Principia Mathematica*, which is not only Newton's masterpiece but also the fundamental work for the whole of modern science.

The mechanics of the *Principia* was an exact quantitative description of the motions of visible bodies. It rested on Newton's three laws of motion: (1) that a body remains in its state of rest unless it is compelled to change that state by a force impressed on it; (2) that the change of motion (the change of velocity times the mass of the body) is proportional to the force impressed; (3) that to every action there is an equal and opposite reaction. The analysis of circular motion in terms of these laws yielded a formula of the quantitative measure, in terms of a body's velocity and mass, of the centripetal force necessary to divert a body from its rectilinear path into a given circle. When Newton substituted this formula into Kepler's third law, he found that the centripetal force holding the planets in their given orbits about the Sun must decrease with the square of the planets' distances from the Sun. Because the satellites of Jupiter also obey Kepler's third law, an inverse square centripetal force must also attract them to the centre of their orbits. Newton was able to show that a similar relation holds between Earth and its Moon. The distance of the Moon is approximately 60 times the radius of Earth. Newton compared the distance by which the Moon, in its orbit of known size, is diverted from a tangential path in one second with the distance that a body at the surface of Earth falls from rest in one second. When the latter distance proved to be 3,600 (60 × 60) times as great as the former, he concluded that one and the same force, governed by a single quantitative law, is operative in all three cases, and from the correlation of the Moon's orbit with the measured acceleration of gravity on the surface of Earth, he applied the ancient Latin word *gravitas* (literally, "heaviness" or "weight") to it. The law of universal gravitation states that every particle of matter in the universe attracts every other particle with a force that is proportional to the product of their masses and inversely proportional to the square of the distance between their centres.

The *Principia* immediately raised Newton to international prominence. In their continuing loyalty to the mechanical ideal, Continental scientists rejected the idea of action at a distance for a generation, but even in their rejection they could not withhold their admiration for the technical expertise revealed by the work. Young British scientists spontaneously recognized him as their model. Within a generation the limited number of salaried positions for scientists in England were monopolized by the young Newtonians of the next generation.

NEWTON'S FINAL YEARS

In the aftermath of the *Principia*, with the great bulk of his creative work completed, Newton was never again satisfied with the academic cloister. In 1696, he was appointed warden of the mint. Although he did not resign his Cambridge appointments until 1701, he moved to London and henceforth centred his life there. As warden and then master of the mint, Newton drew a large income, as much as £2,000 per annum. Added to his personal estate, the income left him a rich man at his death. The position, regarded as a sinecure, was treated otherwise by Newton. During the great recoinage, there was need for him to be actively in command; even afterward, however, he chose to exercise himself in the office. Above all, he was interested in counterfeiting. He became the terror of London counterfeiters, sending a goodly number to the gallows.

In London, Newton assumed the role of patriarch of English science. In 1703 he was elected president of the

Royal Society. Four years earlier, the French Académie des Sciences (Academy of Sciences) had named him one of eight foreign associates. In 1705 Queen Anne knighted him, the first occasion on which a scientist was so honoured.

During his final years he brought out further editions of his central works. The second edition of the *Principia*, edited by Roger Cotes in 1713, introduced extensive alterations. A third edition, edited by Henry Pemberton in 1726, added little more. Until nearly the end, Newton ruled the Royal Society magisterially (frequently dozing through the meetings). His niece, Catherine Barton Conduitt, and her husband lived with him until his death.

CHRISTIAAN HUYGENS

(b. April 14, 1629, The Hague—d. July 8, 1695, The Hague)

Christiaan Huygens (also spelled Christian Huyghens) was a Dutch mathematician, astronomer, and physicist who founded the wave theory of light, discovered the true shape of the rings of Saturn, and made original contributions to the science of dynamics—the study of the action of forces on bodies.

Huygens was from a wealthy and distinguished middle-class family. His father, Constantijn Huygens, a diplomat, Latinist, and poet, was the friend and correspondent of many outstanding intellectual figures of the day, including the scientist and philosopher René Descartes. From an early age, Huygens showed a marked mechanical bent and a talent for drawing and mathematics. Some of his early efforts in geometry impressed Descartes, who was an occasional visitor to the Huygens' household. In 1645 Huygens entered the University of Leiden, where he studied mathematics and law. Two years later he entered the College of Breda, in the midst of a furious controversy

Christiaan Huygens, shown contemplating his work as he constructs the first pendulum clock. Huygens also is noted for founding the wave theory of light and discoveries in the field of dynamics. Three Lions/ Hulton Archive/Getty Images

over the philosophy of Descartes. Although Huygens later rejected certain of the Cartesian tenets including the identification of extension and body, he always affirmed that mechanical explanations were essential in science, a fact that later was to have an important influence on his mathematical interpretation of both light and gravitation.

In 1655 Huygens for the first time visited Paris, where his distinguished parentage, wealth, and affable disposition gave him entry to the highest intellectual and social circles. During his next visit to Paris in 1660, he met Blaise Pascal, with whom he had already been in correspondence on mathematical problems. Huygens had already acquired a European reputation by his publications in mathematics, especially his *De Circuli Magnitudine Inventa* of 1654, and by his discovery in 1659 of the true shape of the rings of Saturn—made possible by the improvements he had introduced in the construction of the telescope with his new method of grinding and polishing lenses. Using his improved telescope, he discovered a satellite of Saturn in March 1655 and distinguished the stellar components of the Orion nebula in 1656. His interest, as an astronomer, in the accurate measurement of time then led him to his discovery of the pendulum as a regulator of clocks, as described in his *Horologium* (1658).

In 1666 Huygens became one of the founding members of the French Academy of Sciences, which granted him a pension larger than that of any other member and an apartment in its building. Apart from occasional visits to Holland, he lived from 1666 to 1681 in Paris, where he made the acquaintance of the German mathematician and philosopher Gottfried Wilhelm Leibniz, with whom he remained on friendly terms for the rest of his life. The major event of Huygens' years in Paris was the publication in 1673 of his *Horologium Oscillatorium*. That brilliant work contained a theory on the mathematics of curvatures, as well as complete solutions to such problems of dynamics as the derivation of the formula for the time of oscillation of the simple pendulum, the oscillation of a body about a stationary axis, and the laws of centrifugal force for uniform circular motion. Some of the results were given without proof in an appendix, and Huygens' complete proofs were not published until after his death.

The treatment of rotating bodies was partly based on an ingenious application of the principle that in any system of bodies the centre of gravity could never rise of its own accord above its initial position. Earlier Huygens had applied the same principle to the treatment of the problem of collisions, for which he had obtained a definitive solution in the case of perfectly elastic bodies as early as 1656, although his results remained unpublished until 1669.

A serious illness in 1681 prompted him to return to Holland, where he intended to stay only temporarily. But the death in 1683 of his patron, Jean-Baptiste Colbert, who had been Louis XIV's chief adviser, and Louis's increasingly reactionary policy, which culminated in the revocation (1685) of the Edict of Nantes, which had granted certain liberties to Protestants, militated against his ever returning to Paris.

Huygens visited London in 1689 and met Sir Isaac Newton and lectured on his own theory of gravitation before the Royal Society. Although he did not engage in public controversy with Newton directly, it is evident from Huygens' correspondence, especially that with Leibniz, that in spite of his generous admiration for the mathematical ingenuity of the *Principia*, he regarded a theory of gravity that was devoid of any mechanical explanation as fundamentally unacceptable. His own theory, published in 1690 in his *Discours de la cause de la pesanteur* ("Discourse on the Cause of Gravity"), though dating at least to 1669, included a mechanical explanation of gravity based on Cartesian vortices. Huygens' *Traité de la Lumière* (*Treatise on Light*), already largely completed by 1678, was also published in 1690. In it he again showed his need for ultimate mechanical explanations in his discussion of the nature of light. But his beautiful explanations of reflection and refraction—far superior to those of Newton—were entirely independent of mechanical explanations, being based solely on the so-called Huygens' principle of secondary wave fronts.

The last five years of Huygens' life were marked by continued ill health and increasing feelings of loneliness and melancholy. He made the final corrections to his will in March 1695 and died after much suffering later that same year.

ROBERT BOYLE

(b. Jan. 25, 1627, Lismore Castle, County Waterford, Ireland—d. Dec. 31, 1691, London)

Robert Boyle was an Anglo-Irish natural philosopher and theological writer, a preeminent figure of 17th-century intellectual culture. He was best known as a natural philosopher, particularly in the field of chemistry, but his scientific work covered many areas including hydrostatics, physics, medicine, earth sciences, natural history, and alchemy. His prolific output also included Christian devotional and ethical essays and theological tracts on biblical language, the limits of reason, and the role of the natural philosopher as a Christian. In 1660 he helped found the Royal Society of London.

EARLY LIFE AND EDUCATION

Boyle was born into one of the wealthiest families in Britain. He was the 14th child and 7th son of Richard

Boyle, the 1st earl of Cork, by his second wife, Catherine, daughter of Sir Geoffrey Fenton, secretary of state for Ireland. At age eight, Boyle began his formal education at Eton College, and in 1639 he and his brother Francis embarked on a grand tour of the continent. In 1642, owing to the Irish rebellion, Francis returned home while Robert remained with his tutor in Geneva and pursued further studies. Boyle returned to England in 1644, where he took up residence at his hereditary estate of Stalbridge in Dorset. There he began a literary career writing ethical and devotional tracts. In 1649 he began investigating nature via scientific experimentation, a process that enthralled him. From 1647 until the mid-1650s, Boyle remained in close contact with a group of natural philosophers and social reformers gathered around the intelligencer Samuel Hartlib. This group included several chemists who heightened Boyle's interest in experimental chemistry.

SCIENTIFIC CAREER

In 1654 Boyle was invited to Oxford, and he took up residence at the university from c. 1656 until 1668. In Oxford he was exposed to the latest developments in natural philosophy and became associated with a group of notable natural philosophers and physicians, including John Wilkins, Christopher Wren, and John Locke. These individuals, together with a few others, formed the "Experimental Philosophy Club," which at times convened in Boyle's lodgings. Much of Boyle's best-known work dates from this period.

In 1659 he and Robert Hooke, the clever inventor and subsequent curator of experiments for the Royal Society, completed the construction of their famous air pump and used it to study pneumatics. Their resultant discoveries regarding air pressure and the vacuum

Coloured portrait of Robert Boyle, the British natural philosopher whose work encompassed many scientific fields. Stock Montage/Archive Photos/ Getty Images

DISCOVERING BOYLE'S LAW

Robert Boyle began his systematic study of air in 1658 after he learned that Otto von Guericke, a German physicist and engineer, had invented an improved air pump four years earlier. From the beginning, he wanted to analyze the elasticity of air quantitatively, not just qualitatively, and to separate the particular experimental problem about air's "spring" from the surrounding philosophical issues. Pouring mercury into the open end of a closed J-shaped tube, Boyle forced the air in the short side of the tube to contract under the pressure of the mercury on top. By doubling the height of the mercury column, he roughly doubled the pressure and halved the volume of air. By tripling the pressure, he cut the volume of air to a third, and so on.

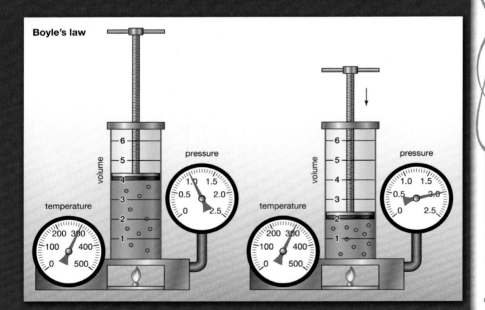

Demonstration of Boyle's law showing that for a given mass, at constant temperature, the pressure times the volume is a constant.
Encyclopædia Britannica, Inc.

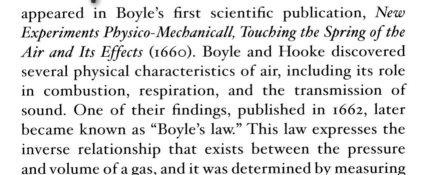

The behaviour of the air under pressure of the mercury can be formulated mathematically in the relation $PV = P'V'$, where P and V are the pressure and volume under one set of conditions and P' and V' represent them under different conditions. In other words, pressure and volume are inversely related for a given quantity of gas. Boyle published his formulation in 1662. Boyle's law was the first physical law ever to be expressed in the form of an equation that describes the functional dependence of two variable quantities.

In France Boyle's law is called Mariotte's law after the physicist Edme Mariotte, who discovered the empirical relationship independently in 1676. Mariotte realized that the law holds true only under constant temperatures; otherwise, the volume of gas expands when heated or contracts when cooled.

appeared in Boyle's first scientific publication, *New Experiments Physico-Mechanicall, Touching the Spring of the Air and Its Effects* (1660). Boyle and Hooke discovered several physical characteristics of air, including its role in combustion, respiration, and the transmission of sound. One of their findings, published in 1662, later became known as "Boyle's law." This law expresses the inverse relationship that exists between the pressure and volume of a gas, and it was determined by measuring the volume occupied by a constant quantity of air when compressed by differing weights of mercury.

Boyle's scientific work is characterized by its reliance on experiment and observation and its reluctance to formulate generalized theories. He advocated a "mechanical philosophy" that saw the universe as a huge machine or clock in which all natural phenomena were accountable purely by mechanical, clockwork motion. His contributions to chemistry were based on a mechanical "corpuscularian hypothesis"—a brand of atomism which claimed that everything was composed of minute (but not indivisible) particles of a single universal matter and that these particles were only differentiable by their shape and motion. Among his most influential writings were *The Sceptical Chymist* (1661), which assailed the then-current Aristotelian and especially Paracelsian notions about the composition of matter and methods of chemical analysis, and the *Origine of Formes and Qualities* (1666), which used chemical phenomena to support the corpuscularian hypothesis.

Boyle also maintained a lifelong pursuit of transmutational alchemy, endeavouring to discover the secret of transmuting base metals into gold and to contact individuals believed to possess alchemical secrets. Overall, Boyle argued so strongly for the need of applying the principles and methods of chemistry to the study of the natural world and to medicine that he later gained the appellation of the father of chemistry.

THEOLOGICAL ACTIVITIES

Boyle was a devout and pious Anglican who keenly championed his faith. He sponsored educational and missionary activities and wrote a number of theological treatises. Whereas the religious writings of Boyle's youth were primarily devotional, his mature works focused on the more complex philosophical issues of reason, nature, and revelation and particularly on the relationship between the emergent new science and religion. Boyle was deeply concerned about the widespread perception that irreligion and atheism were on the rise, and he strove to demonstrate ways in which science and religion were mutually supportive. For Boyle, studying nature as a product of God's handiwork was an inherently religious duty. He argued that this method of study would, in return, illuminate God's omnipresence and goodness, thereby enhancing a scientist's understanding of the divine. *The Christian Virtuoso* (1690) summarized these views and may be seen as a manifesto of Boyle's own life as the model of a Christian scientist.

MATURE YEARS IN LONDON

In 1668 Boyle left Oxford and took up residence with his sister Katherine Jones, Vicountess Ranelagh, in her house on Pall Mall in London. There he set up an active laboratory, employed assistants, received visitors, and published at least one book nearly every year. Living in London also provided him the opportunity to participate actively in the Royal Society. He was offered the presidency of the Royal Society (in 1680) and the episcopacy but declined both. He died at age 64 after a short illness exacerbated by his grief over Katherine's death a week earlier. He left his papers to the Royal Society and a bequest for establishing a series of lectures in defense of Christianity. These lectures, now known as the Boyle Lectures, continue to this day.

Chapter 4

Anatomists, Physicians, and Microscopists

In 1543, the same year as Copernicus's great volume, there appeared an equally important book on anatomy: Andreas Vesalius's *De humani corporis fabrica* ("On the Fabric of the Human Body"), a work in which Vesalius drew on his own studies to correct many errors dating from the Classical era. Vesalius, like Newton a century later, emphasized phenomena, i.e., the accurate description of natural facts. His work was part of a flurry of work in Italy and elsewhere that established anatomy and physiology as sciences in their own right. The work of the great anatomists, physicians, and microscopists profiled in this chapter demonstrated that organic phenomena, like the physical phenomena of inanimate objects in motion, could be studied experimentally.

MONDINO DEI LIUCCI

(b. c. 1270, Bologna, Italy—d. c. 1326, Bologna)

Raimondino Dei Liucci (also called Mondino De Luzzi, or Mundinus) was an Italian physician and anatomist whose *Anathomia Mundini* (MS. 1316; first printed in 1478) was the first European book written since classical antiquity that was entirely devoted to anatomy and was based on the dissection of human cadavers. It remained a standard text until the time of the Flemish anatomist Andreas Vesalius (1514–64).

Mondino received his medical training at the University of Bologna, and after graduation he studied and taught anatomy and surgery at that university while actively practicing medicine and surgery. Mondino was the first to reintroduce the systematic teaching of anatomy into the medical curriculum after this practice had been abandoned for many centuries. He himself performed dissections at public lectures. Mondino's *Anathomia* became the standard handbook for the dissector, going through 39 editions in all. The work followed the anatomical teachings of Galen slavishly, and its descriptions of internal organs were sometimes inaccurate, but it inaugurated a new era in the dissemination of anatomical knowledge.

PARACELSUS

(b. Nov. 11 or Dec. 17, 1493, Einsieeln, Switzerland—d. Sept. 24, 1541, Salzburg, Archbishopric of Salzburg [now in Austria])

Philippus Aureolus Theophrastus Bombastus Von Hohenheim, known through his writings as Paracelsus, was a German-Swiss physician and alchemist who established the role of chemistry in medicine. He published *Der grossen Wundartzney* (*Great Surgery Book*) in 1536 and a clinical description of syphilis in 1530.

EDUCATION

Paracelsus, who was known as Theophrastus when he was a boy, was the only son of an impoverished German doctor and chemist. At the Bergschule in Villach in southern Austria, the youngster learned of metals that "grow" in the earth, watched the transformations of metallic constituents in smelting vats, and perhaps wondered about the transmutation of lead into gold—a conversion believed to be possible by the alchemists of the time. Those experiences gave Paracelsus insight into metallurgy and chemistry, which likely laid the foundations of his later remarkable discoveries in the field of chemotherapy.

In 1507 Paracelsus joined the many wandering youths who traveled throughout Europe in the late Middle Ages, seeking famous teachers at one university after another. Paracelsus is said to have attended the Universities of Basel, Tübingen, Vienna, Wittenberg, Leipzig, Heidelberg, and Cologne during the next five years but was disappointed with them all. "The universities do not teach all things," he wrote, "so a doctor must seek out old wives, gipsies, sorcerers, wandering tribes, old robbers, and such outlaws and take lessons from them. A doctor must be a traveller.... Knowledge is experience." Paracelsus held that the crude language of the innkeeper, the barber, and the teamster had more real dignity and common sense than the dry scholasticism of Aristotle, Galen of Pergamum, and Avicenna, the recognized Greek and Arab medical authorities of his day.

Paracelsus is said to have graduated from the University of Vienna with a baccalaureate in medicine in 1510. He then went to the University of Ferrara in Italy, where it is believed that he received a doctoral degree in 1516, and he is presumed to have begun using the name "para-Celsus" (above or beyond Celsus) at about this time as well. His new name reflected the fact that he regarded himself as even greater than Aulus Cornelius Celsus, a renowned 1st-century Roman medical writer.

CAREER

Soon after taking his degree, he set out upon many years of wandering through almost every country in Europe. He

Portrait of Paracelsus, who pioneered the use of chemistry in the practice of medicine. Paracelsus was also a proponent of natural healing and what has now become known as homeopathic medicine. Hulton Archive/Getty Images

took part in the "Netherlandish wars" as an army surgeon. Later he went to Russia, was held captive by the Tatars, escaped into Lithuania, and went south into Hungary. In 1521 he again served as an army surgeon in Italy. His wanderings eventually took him to Egypt, Arabia, the Holy Land, and, finally, Constantinople. Everywhere he went, he sought out the most learned exponents of practical alchemy, not only to discover the most effective means of medical treatment but also—and even more important—to discover "the latent forces of Nature," and how to use them.

In 1524 Paracelsus returned to his home in Villach to find that his fame for many miraculous cures had preceded him. He was subsequently appointed town physician and lecturer in medicine at the University of Basel in Switzerland, and students from all parts of Europe went to the city to hear his lectures.

On June 5, 1527, he pinned a program of his forthcoming lectures to the notice board of the university, inviting not only students but anyone and everyone to attend, and on June 24, 1527, he reportedly burned the books of Avicenna and Galen in front of the university. These actions incensed the local authorities and recalled in many peoples' minds the German religious reformer Martin Luther, who had circulated his *Theses on Indulgences* and burned a papal bull in a similar manner. Paracelsus seemingly remained a Catholic to his death; however, it is suspected that his books were placed on the *Index Expurgatorius*, a catalogue of books from which passages of text considered immoral or against the Catholic religion are removed.

Paracelsus reached the peak of his career at Basel. In his lectures, he stressed the healing power of nature and denounced the use of methods of treating wounds, such as padding with moss or dried dung, that prevented natural draining. The wounds must drain, he insisted, for "if you prevent infection, Nature will heal the wound all by herself." He also attacked many other medical malpractices of his time, including the use of worthless pills, salves, infusions, balsams, electuaries, fumigants, and drenches.

However, by the spring of 1528 Paracelsus had fallen into disrepute with local doctors, apothecaries, and magistrates. He left Basel, heading first toward Colmar in Upper Alsace. He stayed at various places with friends and continued to travel for the next eight years. During this time, he revised old manuscripts and wrote new treatises. With the publication of *Der grossen Wundartzney* (*Great Surgery Book*) in 1536 he restored, and even extended, the revered reputation he had earned at Basel. He became wealthy and was sought by royalty. In 1541, at the zenith of that second period of renown, Paracelsus died in mysterious circumstances at the White Horse Inn, Salzburg, where he had taken up an appointment under the prince-archbishop, Duke Ernst of Bavaria.

CONTRIBUTIONS TO MEDICINE

In 1530 Paracelsus wrote a clinical description of syphilis, in which he maintained that the disease could be successfully treated by carefully measured doses of mercury compounds taken internally. He stated that the "miners' disease" (silicosis) resulted from inhaling metal vapours and was not a punishment for sin administered by mountain spirits. He was the first to declare that, if given in small doses, "what makes a man ill also cures him"—an anticipation of the modern practice of homeopathy. He was the first to connect goitre with minerals, especially lead, in drinking water.

Paracelsus prepared and used new chemical remedies, including those containing mercury, sulfur, iron, and copper sulfate, thus uniting medicine with chemistry, as the first *London Pharmacopoeia*, in 1618, indicates. Paracelsus, in fact, contributed substantially to the rise of modern medicine, including psychiatric treatment. Swiss psychologist Carl Jung wrote of him that "we see in Paracelsus not only a pioneer in the domains of chemical medicine, but also in those of an empirical psychological healing science."

GIROLAMO FRACASTORO

(b. c. 1478, Verona, Republic of Venice [now in Italy]—d. Aug. 8, 1553, Caffi [now Affi], near Verona)

Girolamo Fracastoro (Latin Hieronymus Fracastorius,) was an Italian physician, poet, astronomer, and geologist who proposed a scientific germ theory of disease more than 300 years before its empirical formulation.

At the University of Padua Fracastoro was a colleague of the astronomer Copernicus. As a physician, he maintained a private practice in Verona. He is best-known for *Syphilis sive morbus Gallicus* (1530; "Syphilis or the French Disease"), a work in rhyme giving an account of the disease, which he named. He made an intense study of epidemic diseases, and, while in the service of Pope Paul III at the Council of Trent (1545–63), he provided the medical justification for the removal of the council to the papal state of Bologna by pointing out the danger of plague in the north Italian town of Trent.

Fracastoro outlined his concept of epidemic diseases in *De contagione et contagiosis morbis* (1546; "On Contagion and Contagious Diseases"), stating that each is caused by a different type of rapidly multiplying minute body and that these bodies are transferred from the infector to the infected in three ways: by direct contact; by carriers such as soiled clothing and linen; and through the air. Although microorganisms had been mentioned as a possible cause of disease by the Roman scholar Marcus

Varro in the 1st century BCE, Fracastoro's was the first scientific statement of the true nature of contagion, infection, disease germs, and modes of disease transmission. Fracastoro's theory was widely praised during his time, but its influence waned, and it fell into general disrepute until an experimental version was later elaborated by German physician Robert Koch and French chemist Louis Pasteur.

AMBROISE PARÉ

(b. 1510, Bourg-Hersent, France—d. Dec. 20, 1590, Paris)

Ambroise Paré was a French physician, one of the most notable surgeons of the European Renaissance, regarded by some medical historians as the father of modern surgery.

About 1533 Paré went to Paris, where he soon became a barber-surgeon apprentice at the Hôtel-Dieu. He was taught anatomy and surgery and in 1537 was employed as an army surgeon. By 1552 he had gained such popularity that he became surgeon to the king; he served four French monarchs: Henry II, Francis II, Charles IX, and Henry III.

At the time Paré entered the army, surgeons treated gunshot wounds with boiling oil since such wounds were believed to be poisonous. On one occasion, when Paré's supply of oil ran out, he treated the wounds with a mixture of egg yolk, rose oil, and turpentine. He found that the wounds he had treated with this mixture were healing better than those treated with the boiling oil. Sometime later he reported his findings in *La Méthod de traicter les playes faites par les arquebuses et aultres bastons à feu* (1545; "The Method of Treating Wounds Made by Harquebuses and Other Guns"), which was ridiculed because it was written in French rather than in Latin. Another of Paré's innovations that did not win immediate medical acceptance was

his reintroduction of the tying of large arteries to replace the method of searing vessels with hot irons to check hemorrhaging during amputation.

Unlike many surgeons of his time, Paré resorted to surgery only when he found it absolutely necessary. He was one of the first surgeons to discard the practice of castrating patients who required surgery for a hernia. He introduced the implantation of teeth, artificial limbs, and artificial eyes made of gold and silver. He invented many scientific instruments, popularized the use of the truss for hernia, and was the first to suggest syphilis as a cause of aneurysm (swelling of blood vessels).

ANDREAS VESALIUS

(b. December 1514, Brussels [now in Belgium]—d. June 1564, island of Zacynthus, Republic of Venice [now in Greece])

Andreas Vesalius (Flemish Andries Van Wesel) was a Renaissance physician who revolutionized the study of biology and the practice of medicine by his careful description of the anatomy of the human body. Basing his observations on dissections he made himself, he wrote and illustrated the first comprehensive textbook of anatomy.

EDUCATION

Vesalius, a native of the duchy of Brabant (the southern portion of which is now in Belgium), was from a family of physicians and pharmacists. He attended the Catholic University of Leuven (Louvain) in 1529–33, and from 1533 to 1536 he studied at the medical school of the University of Paris, where he learned to dissect animals. He also had the opportunity to dissect human cadavers, and he devoted much of his time to a study of human bones, at that time easily available in the Paris cemeteries.

In 1536 Vesalius returned to Brabant to spend another year at the Catholic University of Leuven, where the influence of Arab medicine was still dominant. Following the prevailing custom, he prepared, in 1537, a paraphrase of the work of the 10th-century Arab physician Rhazes, probably in fulfillment of the requirements for the bachelor of medicine degree. He then went to the University of Padua, a progressive university with a strong tradition of anatomical dissection. On receiving the M.D. degree the same year, he was appointed a lecturer in surgery with the responsibility of giving anatomical demonstrations. Since he knew that a thorough knowledge of human anatomy was essential to surgery, he devoted much of his time to dissections of cadavers and insisted on doing them himself, instead of relying on untrained assistants.

THE *FABRICA*

At first, Vesalius had no reason to question the theories of Galen, the Greek physician who had served the emperor Marcus Aurelius in Rome and whose books on anatomy were still considered as authoritative in medical education in Vesalius's time. In January 1540, breaking with this tradition of relying on Galen, Vesalius openly demonstrated his own method—doing dissections himself, learning anatomy from cadavers, and critically evaluating ancient texts. He did so while visiting the University of Bologna. Such methods soon convinced him that Galenic anatomy had not been based on the dissection of the human body, which had been strictly forbidden by the Roman religion. Galenic anatomy, he maintained, was an application to the human form of conclusions drawn from the dissections of

Woodcut from Andreas Vesalius's On the Fabric of the Human Body, *showing the author dissecting the arm of a human cadaver.* Science & Society Picture Library/Getty Images

animals, mostly dogs, monkeys, or pigs. It was this conclusion that he had the audacity to declare in his teaching as he hurriedly prepared his complete textbook of human anatomy for publication. Early in 1542 he traveled to Venice to supervise the preparation of drawings to illustrate his text, probably in the studio of the great Renaissance artist Titian. The drawings of his dissections were engraved on wood blocks, which he took, together with his manuscript, to Basel, Switz., where his major work *De humani corporis fabrica* ("On the Fabric of the Human Body"), commonly known as the *Fabrica*, was printed in 1543.

In this epochal work, Vesalius deployed all his scientific, humanistic, and aesthetic gifts. The *Fabrica* was a more extensive and accurate description of the human body than any put forward by his predecessors. It gave anatomy a new language, and, in the elegance of its printing and organization, a perfection hitherto unknown.

CAREER

Early in 1543, Vesalius left for Mainz, to present his book to the Holy Roman emperor Charles V, who engaged him as regular physician to the household. Thus, when not yet 28 years old, Vesalius had attained his goal. After relinquishing his post in Padua, and returning in the spring of 1544 to his native land to marry Anne van Hamme, he took up new duties in the service of the emperor on his travels in Europe. From 1553 to 1556 Vesalius spent most of his time in Brussels, where he built an imposing house in keeping with his growing affluence and attended to his flourishing medical practice. His prestige was further enhanced when Charles V, on abdication from the Spanish throne in 1556, provided him with a lifetime pension and made him a count.

Vesalius went to Spain in 1559 with his wife and daughter to take up an appointment, made by Philip II, son of Charles V, as one of the physicians in the Madrid court. In 1564 Vesalius obtained permission to leave Spain to go on pilgrimage to the Holy Sepulchre. He traveled to Jerusalem, with stops at Venice and Cyprus, his wife and daughter having returned to Brussels. Conflicting reports obscure the final days of Vesalius's life. Apparently he became ill aboard ship while returning to Europe from his pilgrimage. He was put ashore on the Greek island of Zacynthus, where he died.

ASSESSMENT

Vesalius's work represented the culmination of the humanistic revival of ancient learning, the introduction of human dissections into medical curricula, and the growth of a European anatomical literature. Vesalius performed his dissections with a thoroughness hitherto unknown. After Vesalius, anatomy became a scientific discipline, with far-reaching implications not only for physiology but for all of biology. During his own lifetime, however, Vesalius found it easier to correct points of Galenic anatomy than to challenge his physiological framework.

GABRIEL FALLOPIUS

(b. 1523, Modena [Italy]—d. Oct. 9, 1562, Padua)

Gabriel Fallopius (Italian Gabriello Fallopio, or Gabriello Fallopia), the most illustrious of 16th-century Italian anatomists, contributed greatly to early knowledge of the ear and of the reproductive organs.

Fallopius served as canon of the cathedral of Modena and then turned to the study of medicine at the University of Ferrara, where he became a teacher of anatomy. He then held positions at the University of Pisa (1548–51) and at Padua (1551–62). His exhaustive observations, made during dissection of human cadavers and outlined in *Observationes anatomicae* (1561), earned him the respect and admiration of his colleagues, including the great Renaissance anatomist Andreas Vesalius.

Fallopius discovered the tubes that connect the ovaries to the uterus (now known as fallopian tubes) and several major nerves of the head and face. He described the semicircular canals of the inner ear (responsible for maintaining body equilibrium) and named the vagina, placenta, clitoris, palate, and cochlea (the snail-shaped organ of hearing in the inner ear). A friend and supporter of Vesalius, he joined him in a vigorous assault on the principles of the classic Greek anatomist Galen, which resulted in a shift of attitude essential to the development of Renaissance medicine.

HIERONYMUS FABRICIUS

(b. May 20, 1537, Acquapendente, Italy—d. May 21, 1619, Padua)

Hieronymus Fabricius ab Aquapendente (Italian Geronimo, or Girolamo, Fabrizio, or Fabrici) was an Italian surgeon and an outstanding Renaissance anatomist who helped found modern embryology.

He spent most of his life at the University of Padua, where he studied under the eminent anatomist Gabriel Fallopius. As Fallopius's successor to the chair of surgery and anatomy (1562–1613), Fabricius built a reputation that attracted students from all of Europe. The English anatomist William Harvey was his pupil. In *De Venarum Ostiolis* (1603; "On the Valves of the Veins"), Fabricius gave the

first clear description of the semilunar valves of the veins, which later provided Harvey with a crucial point in his famous argument for circulation of the blood.

Fabricius's *De Formato Foetu* (1600; "On the Formation of the Fetus"), summarizing his investigations of the fetal development of many animals, including man, contained the first detailed description of the placenta and opened the field of comparative embryology. He also gave the first full account of the larynx as a vocal organ and was first to demonstrate that the pupil of the eye changes its size.

SANTORIO SANTORIO

(b. March 29, 1561, Capodistria [now Koper, Slovenia]—d. Feb. 22, 1636, Venice)

Santorio Santorio (Latin Sanctorius, or Santorius) was an Italian physician who was the first to employ instruments of precision in the practice of medicine and whose studies of basal metabolism introduced quantitative experimental procedure into medical research.

Santorio was a graduate of the University of Padua (M.D., 1582), where he later became professor of medical theory (1611–24). About 1587 he was apparently summoned to attend as physician on a Croatian nobleman. From 1587 to 1599 Santorio seems to have spent much time among the southern Slavs, though he maintained a frequent correspondence with his Paduan colleagues, the astronomer Galileo Galilei and the anatomist Hieronymus Fabricius. Santorio was an early exponent of the iatrophysical school of medicine, which attempted to explain the workings of the animal body on purely mechanical grounds, and he adapted several of Galileo's inventions to medical practice, resulting in his development of a clinical thermometer (1612) and a pulse clock (1602).

Endeavouring to test the Greek physician Galen's assertion that respiration also occurs through the skin as "insensible perspiration," Santorio constructed a large scale on which he frequently ate, worked, and slept, so that he might study the fluctuations of his body weight in relation to his solid and liquid excretions. After 30 years of continuous experimentation, he found that the sum total of visible excreta was less than the amount of substance ingested. His *De Statica Medicina* (1614; "On Medical Measurement") was the first systematic study of basal metabolism.

WILLIAM HARVEY

(b. April 1, 1578, Folkestone, Kent, England—d. June 3, 1657, London)

William Harvey was an English physician who was the first to recognize the full circulation of the blood in the human body and to provide experiments and arguments to support this idea.

EDUCATION AND CAREER

Harvey had seven brothers and two sisters, and his father, Thomas Harvey, was a farmer and landowner. Harvey attended the King's School in Canterbury, Kent, from 1588 to 1593 and went on to study arts and medicine at Gonville and Caius College, Cambridge, from 1593 to 1599. He continued his studies at the University of Padua, the leading European medical school at the time. He became a student of Italian anatomist and surgeon Hieronymous Fabricius, who had a considerable influence on Harvey. It is also likely that Harvey was taught by Italian philosopher Cesare Cremonini, a prominent follower of Aristotle.

Harvey earned his doctorate from Padua on April 25, 1602, and then returned to England to work as a doctor. In 1604 he married Elizabeth Browne, the daughter of Launcelot Browne, a London physician, who served as physician to James I, the king of England and Scotland. Harvey and his wife appear to have been happy together, and Harvey referred to her as "my dear deceased loving wife" in his will. However, they did not have any children. Harvey was a fellow of the Royal College of Physicians of London from 1607 and was active in this society for the remainder of his life. In 1609 he was appointed physician at St. Bartholomew's Hospital, a post he held until 1643, when the parliamentary authorities in London had him replaced, Harvey being a staunch supporter of the monarchy.

PHYSICIAN TO THE KING

Harvey was appointed physician to James I in 1618 and continued as physician to Charles I upon Charles's accession to the throne in 1625. Harvey built a considerable practice in this period, tending to many important men, including author and philosopher Sir Francis Bacon. In 1625 Harvey led the group of doctors attending James during his last illness and was an important witness in the trial of George Villiers, duke of Buckingham, who was accused of poisoning the king. Harvey was rewarded by Charles I for his care of James. Charles and Harvey seem to have enjoyed an amicable relationship, Harvey being allowed to experiment on the royal herd of deer and presenting interesting medical cases to the king.

In 1636 Harvey acted as doctor to a diplomatic mission sent to see the Holy Roman emperor, Ferdinand II. This involved nearly a year of travel around Europe. He met renowned German professor of medicine Casper

British physician William Harvey (left), *shown presenting his latest theory before King Charles I, with whom Harvey had a congenial relationship.* NYPL/Science Source/Photo Researchers/Getty Images

Hofmann at Nürnberg and attempted to demonstrate the circulation of the blood to him. Harvey also had a wide interest in philosophy, literature, and art. During the diplomatic mission of 1636 he visited Italy to look for paintings for the royal collection. He was friends with Robert Fludd, an important English physician and philosopher whose primary interest concerned natural magic, and Thomas Hobbes, a famous political philosopher. He was also acquainted with John Aubrey, the 17th-century biographer, who gave an account of Harvey in his manuscript *Brief Lives*.

Harvey was a committed royalist. He followed the king on the Scottish campaigns of 1639, 1640, and 1641, was with him from 1642 to 1646 during the English Civil Wars, and was even present at the Battle of Edgehill in 1642. His political views may be judged from the dedication to the king in his most important book, *De Motu Cordis* (1628):

> *Most serene King! The animal's heart is the basis of its life, its chief member, the sun of its microcosm; on the heart all its activity depends, from the heart all its liveliness and strength arise. Equally is the king the basis of his kingdoms, the sun of his microcosm, the heart of the state; from him all power arises and all grace stems.*

Harvey attended Charles in Oxford during the Civil Wars and in Newcastle when the king was held in captivity. Harvey eventually returned to London, in 1647.

LATER LIFE

In Harvey's later life, he suffered from gout, kidney stones, and insomnia. In 1651, following the publication of his final work, *Exercitationes de Generatione Animalium* (*Exercises on the Generation of Animals*), it is believed that Harvey attempted to take his own life with laudanum (an alcoholic tincture of opium). However, this attempt failed. On June 3, 1657, at the age of 79, he died of a stroke.

DISCOVERY OF CIRCULATION

Harvey's key work was *Exercitatio Anatomica de Motu Cordis et Sanguinis in Animalibus* (*Anatomical Exercise on*

THE INVENTION OF THE MICROSCOPE

The concept of magnification has long been known. About 1267 English philosopher Roger Bacon wrote in *Perspectiva*, "[We] may number the smallest particles of dust and sand by reason of the greatness of the angle under which we may see them," and in 1538 Italian physician Girolamo Fracastoro wrote in *Homocentrica*, "If anyone should look through two spectacle glasses, one being superimposed on the other, he will see everything much larger."

Three Dutch spectacle makers—Hans Jansen, his son Zacharias Jansen, and Hans Lippershey—have received credit for inventing the compound microscope about 1590. The first portrayal of a microscope was drawn about 1631 in the Netherlands. It was clearly of a compound microscope, with an eyepiece and an objective lens. This kind of instrument, which came to be made of wood and cardboard, often adorned with polished fish skin, became increasingly popular in the mid-17th century and was used by the English natural philosopher Robert Hooke to provide regular demonstrations for the new Royal Society. These demonstrations commenced in 1663, and two years later Hooke published a folio volume titled *Micrographia*, which introduced a wide range of microscopic views of familiar objects (fleas, lice, and nettles among them). In this book he coined the term "cell."

Hidden in the unnumbered pages of *Micrographia*'s preface is a description of how a single high-powered lens could be made into a serviceable microscope, and it was using this design that the Dutch civil servant Antonie van Leeuwenhoek began his pioneering observations of freshwater microorganisms in the 1670s. He made his postage-stamp-sized microscopes by hand, and the best of them could resolve details around 0.7 micrometres (0.7 millionth of a metre). His fine specimens discovered in excellent condition at the Royal Society more than three centuries later prove what a great technician he was. Using his simple microscope, Leeuwenhoek effectively launched microbiology in 1674, and single-lensed microscopes remained popular until the 1850s. In 1827 they were used by Scottish botanist Robert Brown to demonstrate the ubiquity of the "cell nucleus," a term he coined in 1831.

the Motion of the Heart and Blood in Animals), published in 1628, with an English version in 1653. Harvey's greatest achievement was to recognize that the blood flows rapidly around the human body, being pumped through a single system of arteries and veins, and to support this hypothesis with experiments and arguments. There had been suggestions, both within the European tradition (by 16th-century Spanish physician Servetus) and within the Islamic tradition (by 13th-century physician Ibn al-Nafīs) of a "lesser circulation," whereby blood circulated from the heart to the lungs and back, without circulating around the whole body.

Prior to Harvey, it was believed there were two separate blood systems in the body. One carried purple, "nutritive" blood and used the veins to distribute nutrition from the liver to the rest of the body. The other carried scarlet, "vivyfying" (or "vital") blood and used the arteries to distribute a life-giving principle from the lungs. Today these blood systems are understood as deoxygenated blood and oxygenated blood. However, at the time, the influence of oxygen on blood was not understood. Furthermore, blood was not thought to circulate around the body—it was believed to be consumed by the body at the same rate that it was produced. The capillaries, small vessels linking the arteries and veins, were unknown at the time, and their existence was not confirmed until later in the 17th century, after Harvey, when the microscope had been invented.

Harvey claimed he was led to his discovery of the circulation by consideration of the venous valves. It was known that there were small flaps inside the veins that allowed free passage of blood in one direction but strongly inhibited the flow of blood in the opposite direction. It was thought that these flaps prevented pooling of the blood under the influence of gravity, but Harvey was able to show that all these flaps are cardiocentrically oriented. For example, he showed that in the jugular vein of the neck they face downward, inhibiting blood flow away from the heart, instead of upward, inhibiting pooling due to gravity.

Harvey's main experiment concerned the amount of blood flowing through the heart. He made estimates of the volume of the ventricles, how efficient they were in expelling blood, and the number of beats per minute made by the heart. He was able to show, even with conservative estimates, that more blood passed through the heart than could possibly be accounted for based on the then current understanding of blood flow. Harvey's values indicated the heart pumped 0.5–1 litre of blood per minute (modern values are about 4 litres per minute at rest and 25 litres per minute during exercise). The human body contains about 5 litres of blood. The body simply could not produce or consume that amount of blood so rapidly; therefore, the blood had to circulate.

It is also important that Harvey investigated the nature of the heartbeat. Prior to Harvey, it was thought that the active phase of the heartbeat, when the muscles contract, was when the heart increased its internal volume. So the active motion of the heart was to draw blood into itself. Harvey observed the heart beating in many animals—particularly in cold-blooded animals and in animals near death, because their heartbeats were slow. He concluded that the active phase of the heartbeat, when the muscles contract, is when the heart decreases its internal volume and that blood is expelled with considerable force from the heart.

Harvey's theory of circulation was opposed by conservative physicians, but it was well established by the time of his death. It is likely that Harvey actually made his discovery of the circulation about 1618–19. Such a major shift in thinking about the body needed to be very well supported by experiment and argument to avoid immediate ridicule and dismissal; hence the delay before the publication of his central work. In 1649 Harvey published *Exercitationes Duae Anatomicae de Circulatione Sanguinis, ad Joannem Riolanem, Filium, Parisiensem* (*Two Anatomical Exercises on the Circulation of the Blood*) in response to criticism of the circulation theory by French anatomist Jean Riolan.

Harvey was very much influenced by the ideas of Greek philosopher Aristotle and the natural magic tradition of the Renaissance. His key analogy for the circulation of the blood was a macrocosm/microcosm analogy with the weather system. Water was changed into vapour by the action of the Sun, and the vapour rose, was cooled, and fell again as rain. The microcosm was the human body, where the action of the heart was supposed to heat and change the blood, which was cooled again in the extremities of the body. Harvey says (and compare the earlier quote concerning the king) that:

> So the heart is the beginning of life, the Sun of the Microcosm, as proportionably the Sun deserves to be call'd the heart of the world, by whose vertue, and pulsation, the blood is mov'd, perfected, made vegetable, and is defended from corruption and mattering;

and this familiar household-god doth his duty to the whole body, by nourishing, cherishing, and vegetating, being the foundation of life, and author of all.

JAN BAPTISTA VAN HELMONT

(b. Jan. 12, 1580 [1579, Old Style], Brussels [Belgium]—d. Dec. 30, 1644, Vilvoorde, Spanish Netherlands [Belgium])

Jan (or Joannes) Baptista van Helmont was a Flemish physician, philosopher, mystic, and chemist who recognized the existence of discrete gases and identified carbon dioxide.

EDUCATION AND EARLY LIFE

Van Helmont was born into a wealthy family of the landed gentry. He studied at Leuven (Louvain), where he finished the course in philosophy and classics, and then flirted with theology, geography, and law before finally taking a doctorate in medicine in 1599. He later referred to his education as "reaping straw and senseless prattle," gave away or threw away his books, and set out to try to find true knowledge. Van Helmont traveled to Switzerland and Italy (1600–02) and to France and England (1602–05), gaining practical medical skills that he put to use during an outbreak of plague in Antwerp in 1605. It was apparently during these sojourns that he came to know and appreciate some of the theories of the German-Swiss physician Paracelsus. He received several offers—from princes, an archbishop, and an emperor—to become a private physician, but he turned them down, refusing to "live on the misery of my fellow men."

In 1609 van Helmont married into a noble family, thereby becoming the manorial lord of several estates. He

retired to one of them—Mérode, in Vilvoorde—and for the next seven years dedicated himself to chemical research and "to the relief of the poor." In fact, he spent his life in relative solitude and mostly in peace. He had several daughters and three sons (two of whom were lost to plague).

PUBLICATIONS

Van Helmont published very little until near the end of his life. This may be explained in part by the fact that his first known publication, "Of the Magnetic Curing of Wounds" (1621), led to trouble with the Spanish Inquisition. In addition to suggesting that saintly relics might display their curative effects through magnetic influence, he included very uncomplimentary comments regarding Jesuit scholastics. As a result, ecclesiastical court proceedings of one sort or another were pending against him for more than 20 years.

Van Helmont also published a treatise on the waters of Spa (1624) that criticized an earlier work and made him some enemies among physicians. Other tracts were issued in 1642 and 1644. At some time shortly before his death, van Helmont gave to his surviving son, Francis Mercurius, the responsibility for publishing all of his writings. The result was *Ortus Medicinæ* (1648; "Origin of Medicine").

MAJOR EXPERIMENTS

Van Helmont was a man of his age and accepted the ideas of spontaneous generation, transmutation of metals, and the existence of a medical panacea. However, he insisted that knowledge of the natural world could be obtained only by experimentation. Many of his treatises deal with the refutation of commonly held views and the experimental evidence for his own views. He rejected the ideas of the four elements (earth, air, water, and fire) of Aristotle and the three principles (salt, mercury, and sulfur) of Paracelsus (as received from Arabic alchemists). For him, the only true elements were air and water, and he demonstrated that these were not interchangeable, as some thought.

In what is perhaps his best-known experiment, van Helmont placed a willow weighting about 5 pounds (2.2 kg) in an earthen pot containing about 200 pounds (90 kg) of dried soil, and over a five-year period he added nothing to the pot but rainwater or distilled water. After five years, he found that the tree weighed about 169 pounds (177 kg), while the soil had lost only 2 ounces (57 grams). He concluded that the added weight "of wood, barks, and roots arose out of water only," and he had not even included the weight of the leaves that fell off every autumn. Obviously, he knew nothing of photosynthesis, in which carbon from the air and minerals from the soil are used to generate new plant tissue, but his use of the balance is important; he believed that the mass of materials had to be accounted for in chemical processes.

OTHER CONTRIBUTIONS

Van Helmont was the first to recognize that many reactions produce substances that are, in his words, "far more subtle or fine...than a vapour, mist, or distilled oiliness, although... many times thicker than air." To describe these substances, he invented the word "gas" (from "chaos") and identified a number of gases, including carbon dioxide. (Ironically, carbon dioxide was the major substance overlooked in his willow tree experiment.) His work on gases was taken up by the British natural philosopher Robert Boyle, among others, and the word gas, after being reintroduced by the 18th-century French chemist Antoine-Laurent Lavoisier, became a standard chemical term.

Through many experiments in physiology, van Helmont demonstrated that acid was the digestive element in the

stomach and was neutralized by alkali in the intestine and that blood combined with a "ferment from the air," with venous blood removing a residue that escaped through the lungs. He studied extensively the formation and nature of kidney stones. His theory of "ferments" as the agents bringing about physiological processes is a crude precursor of the idea of enzymes.

GIOVANNI ALFONSO BORELLI

(b. Jan. 28, 1608, Naples, Kingdom of Naples [Italy]—d. Dec. 31, 1679, Rome)

Giovanni Alfonso Borelli (original name Giovanni Francesco Antonio Alonso) was an Italian physiologist and physicist who was the first to explain muscular movement and other body functions according to the laws of statics and dynamics.

He was appointed professor of mathematics at Messina in 1649 and at Pisa in 1656. In 1667 he returned to Messina and in 1674 went to Rome, where he lived under the protection of Christina, former queen of Sweden. His best-known work is *De Motu Animalium* (1680–81; "On the Movement of Animals"), in which he sought to explain the movements of the animal body on mechanical principles; he thus ranks as the founder of the iatrophysical school.

Borelli also wrote many astronomical works, including a treatise in 1666 that considered the influence of attraction on the satellites of Jupiter. In a letter published in 1665 under the pseudonym Pier Maria Mutoli, he was the first to suggest the idea that comets travel in a parabolic path.

FRANCISCUS SYLVIUS

(b. March 15, 1614, Hanau, Germany—d. Nov. 15, 1672, Leiden, Netherlands)

Franciscus Sylvius (German Franz de le Boë; French François du Bois) was a physician, physiologist, anatomist, and chemist who is considered the founder of the 17th-century iatrochemical school of medicine, which held that all phenomena of life and disease are based on chemical action. His studies helped shift medical emphasis from mystical speculation to a rational application of universal laws of physics and chemistry.

Basing his medical system on the recent discovery of the circulation of the blood by the English anatomist William Harvey, while keeping it within the general framework of the classic Greek physician Galen's humoral theories, Sylvius felt that the most important processes of normal and pathological life take place in the blood and that diseases should be explained and treated chemically. Recognizing the existence of salts in living matter, he concluded that they were the result of an interaction of acids and bases; thus, he postulated that chemical imbalances consist of either an excess of acid (acidosis) or an excess of alkali (alkalosis) in the blood, and he devised drugs to counteract these conditions.

A professor of medicine at the University of Leiden (1658–72), Sylvius was one of Europe's outstanding teachers. He was among the first to introduce ward instruction in medical education, and he instigated the construction of perhaps the first university chemistry laboratory. He was the first to distinguish between two kinds of glands: conglomerate (made up of a number of smaller units, the excretory ducts of which combine to form ducts of progressively higher order) and conglobate (forming a rounded mass, or clump). He also discovered (1641) the deep cleft (Sylvian fissure) separating the temporal (lower), frontal, and parietal (top rear) lobes of the brain.

MARCELLO MALPIGHI

(b. March 10, 1628, Crevalcore, near Bologna, Papal States [Italy]—d. Nov. 30, 1694, Rome)

Marcello Malpighi was an Italian physician and biologist who, in developing experimental methods to study living things, founded the science of microscopic anatomy. After Malpighi's researches, microscopic anatomy became a prerequisite for advances in the fields of physiology, embryology, and practical medicine.

LIFE

Little is known of Malpighi's childhood and youth except that his father had him engage in "grammatical studies" at an early age and that he entered the University of Bologna in 1646. Both parents died when he was 21, but he was able, nevertheless, to continue his studies. Despite opposition from the university authorities because he was non-Bolognese by birth, in 1653 he was granted doctorates in both medicine and philosophy and appointed as a teacher, whereupon he immediately dedicated himself to further study in anatomy and medicine.

In 1656, Ferdinand II of Tuscany invited him to the professorship of theoretical medicine at the University of Pisa. There Malpighi began his lifelong friendship with Giovanni Borelli, mathematician and naturalist, who was a prominent supporter of the Accademia del Cimento, one of the first scientific societies. Malpighi questioned the prevailing medical teachings at Pisa, tried experiments on colour changes in blood, and attempted to recast anatomical, physiological, and medical problems of the day. Family responsibilities and poor health prompted Malpighi's return in 1659 to the University of Bologna, where he continued to teach and do research with his microscopes. In

1661 he identified and described the pulmonary and capillary network connecting small arteries with small veins, one of the major discoveries in the history of science. Malpighi's views evoked increasing controversy and dissent, mainly from envy, jealousy, and lack of understanding on the part of his colleagues.

Hindered by the hostile environment of Bologna, Malpighi accepted (November 1662) a professorship in medicine at the University of Messina in Sicily, on the recommendation there of Borelli, who was investigating the effects of physical forces on animal functions. Malpighi was also welcomed by Visconte Giacomo Ruffo Francavilla, a patron of science and a former student, whose hospitality encouraged him in furthering his career. Malpighi pursued his microscopic studies while teaching and practicing medicine. He identified the taste buds and regarded them as terminations of nerves, described the minute structure of the brain, optic nerve, and fat reservoirs, and in 1666 was the first to see the red blood cells and to attribute the colour of blood to them. Again, his research and teaching aroused envy and controversy among his colleagues.

After four years at Messina, Malpighi returned in January 1667 to Bologna, where, during his medical practice, he studied the microscopic subdivisions of specific living organs, such as the liver, brain, spleen, and kidneys, and of bone and the deeper layers of the skin that now bear his name. Impressed by the minute structures he observed under the microscope, he concluded that most living materials are glandular in organization, that even the largest organs are composed of minute glands, and that these glands exist solely for the separation or for the mixture of juices.

Malpighi's work at Messina had attracted the attention of the Royal Society of London, whose secretary, Henry Oldenburg, extended him an invitation in 1668 to

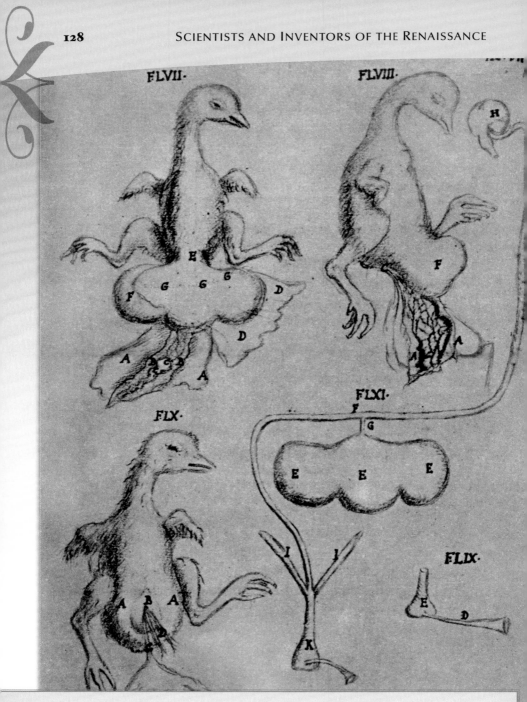

Marcello Malpighi's sketches showing the embryological development of chickens. NYPL/Science Source/Photo Researchers/Getty Images

correspond with him. Malpighi's work was thereafter published periodically in the form of letters in the *Philosophical Transactions* of the Royal Society. In 1669 Malpighi was named an honorary member, the first such recognition given to an Italian. From then on, all his works were published in London.

At the peak of his fame, Malpighi could have left his tiring medical practice and research to accept one of the many highly remunerative positions offered to him. Instead, he chose to continue his general practice and professorship. His years at Bologna marked the climax of his career, when he marked out large areas of microscopy. Malpighi conducted many studies of insect larvae — establishing, in so doing, the basis for their future study — the most important of which was his investigation in 1669 of the structure and development of the silkworm. In his historic work in 1673 on the embryology of the chick, he discovered the aortic arches, neural folds, and somites. He also made extensive comparative studies in 1675–79 of the microscopic anatomy of several different plants and saw an analogy between plant and animal organization.

During the last decade of his life Malpighi was beset by personal tragedy, declining health, and the climax of opposition to him. In 1684 his villa was burned, his apparatus and microscopes shattered, and his papers, books, and manuscripts destroyed. Most probably as a compensatory move when opposition mounted against his views, and in recognition of his stature, Pope Innocent XII invited him to Rome in 1691 as papal archiater, or personal physician, such a nomination constituting a great honour. In Rome he was further honoured by being named a count, he was elected to the College of Doctors of Medicine, his name was placed in the Roman Patriciate Roll, and he was given the title of honorary valet.

ASSESSMENT

Malpighi may be regarded as the first histologist. For almost 40 years he used the microscope to describe the major types of plant and animal structures and in so doing marked out for future generations of biologists major areas of research in botany, embryology, human anatomy, and pathology. Just as Galileo had applied the new technical achievement of the optical lens to vistas beyond Earth, Malpighi extended its use to the intricate organization of living things, hitherto unimagined, below the level of unaided sight. Moreover, his lifework brought into question the prevailing concepts of body function. When, for example, he found that the blood passed through the capillaries, it meant that Harvey was right, that blood was not transformed into flesh in the periphery, as the ancients thought. He was vigorously denounced by his enemies, who failed to see how his many discoveries, such as the renal glomeruli, urinary tubules, dermal papillae, taste buds, and the glandular components of the liver, could possibly improve medical practice. Although Malpighi could not say what new remedies might come from his discoveries, he was convinced that microscopic anatomy, by showing the minute construction of living things, called into question the value of old medicine. He provided the anatomical basis for the eventual understanding of human physiological exchanges.

THOMAS WILLIS

(b. Jan. 27, 1621, Great Bedwyn, Wiltshire, England—d. Nov. 11, 1675, London)

Thomas Willis was a British physician, a leader of the English iatrochemists, who attempted to explain the workings of the body from current knowledge of chemical interactions; he is known for his careful studies of the nervous system and of various diseases. An Oxford professor of natural philosophy (1660–75), he opened a London practice in 1666 that became the most fashionable and profitable of the period.

In his *Cerebri Anatome, cui accessit Nervorum descriptio et usus* (1664; "Anatomy of the Brain, with a Description of the Nerves and Their Function"), the most complete and accurate account of the nervous system to that time, he rendered the first description of the hexagonal continuity of arteries (the circle of Willis) located at the base of the brain and ensuring that organ a maximum blood supply, and of the 11th cranial nerve, or spinal accessory nerve, responsible for motor stimulation of major neck muscles. Willis also was first to describe myasthenia gravis (1671), a chronic muscular fatigue marked by progressive paralysis, and puerperal (childbed) fever, which he named.

ROBERT HOOKE

(b. July 18, 1635, Freshwater, Isle of Wight, England—d. March 3, 1703, London)

The English physicist Robert Hooke discovered the law of elasticity, known as Hooke's law, and did research in a remarkable variety of fields.

In 1655 Hooke was employed by Robert Boyle to construct the Boylean air pump. Five years later, Hooke discovered his law of elasticity, which states that the stretching of a solid body (e.g., metal, wood) is proportional to the force applied to it. The law laid the basis for studies of stress and strain and for understanding of elastic materials. He applied these studies in his designs for the balance springs of watches. In 1662 he was appointed curator of experiments to the Royal Society of London and was elected a fellow the following year.

One of the first men to build a Gregorian reflecting telescope, Hooke discovered the fifth star in the Trapezium, an asterism in the constellation Orion, in 1664 and first suggested that Jupiter rotates on its axis. His detailed sketches of Mars were used in the 19th century to determine that planet's rate of rotation. In 1665 he was appointed professor of geometry in Gresham College.

In *Micrographia* (1665; "Small Drawings") he included his studies and illustrations of the crystal structure of snowflakes, discussed the possibility of manufacturing artificial fibres by a process similar to the spinning of the silkworm, and first used the word "cell" to name the microscopic honeycomb cavities in cork. His studies of microscopic fossils led him to become one of the first proponents of a theory of evolution.

He suggested that the force of gravity could be measured by utilizing the motion of a pendulum (1666) and attempted to show that Earth and the Moon follow an elliptical path around the Sun. In 1672 he discovered the phenomenon of diffraction (the bending of light rays around corners); to explain it, he offered the wave theory of light. He stated the inverse square law to describe planetary motions in 1678, a law that Newton later used in modified form. Hooke complained that he was not given sufficient credit for the law and became involved in bitter controversy with Newton. Hooke was the first man to state in general that all matter expands when heated and that air is made up of particles separated from each other by relatively large distances.

ANTONIE VAN LEEUWENHOEK

(b. Oct. 24, 1632, Delft, Netherlands—d. Aug. 26, 1723, Delft)
Antonie van Leeuwenhoek was a Dutch microscopist who was the first to observe bacteria and protozoa.

His researches on lower animals refuted the doctrine of spontaneous generation, and his observations helped lay the foundations for the sciences of bacteriology and protozoology.

Little is known of Leeuwenhoek's early life. When his stepfather died in 1648, he was sent to Amsterdam to become an apprentice to a linendraper. Returning to Delft when he was 20, he established himself as a draper and haberdasher. In 1660 he obtained a position as chamberlain to the sheriffs of Delft. His income was thus secure and sufficient enough to enable him to devote much of his time to his all-absorbing hobby, that of grinding lenses and using them to study tiny objects.

Leeuwenhoek made microscopes consisting of a single, high-quality lens of very short focal length; at the time, such simple microscopes were preferable to the compound microscope, which increased the problem of chromatic aberration. Although Leeuwenhoek's studies lacked the organization of formal scientific research, his powers of careful observation enabled him to make discoveries of fundamental importance. In 1674 he began to observe bacteria and protozoa, his "very little animalcules," which he was able to isolate from different sources, such as rainwater, pond and well water, and the human mouth and intestine, and he calculated their sizes.

In 1677 he described for the first time the spermatozoa from insects, dogs, and man, though Stephen Hamm probably was a codiscoverer. Leeuwenhoek studied the structure of the optic lens, striations in muscles, the mouthparts of insects, and the fine structure of plants and discovered parthenogenesis in aphids. In 1680 he noticed that yeasts consist of minute globular particles. He extended Marcello Malpighi's demonstration in 1660 of the blood capillaries by giving (in 1684) the first accurate description of red blood cells. In his observations on rotifers in 1702, Leeuwenhoek remarked that "in all falling rain, carried from gutters into water-butts, animalcules are to be found; and that in all kinds of water, standing in the open air, animalcules can turn up. For these animalcules can be carried over by the wind, along with the bits of dust floating in the air."

A friend of Leeuwenhoek put him in touch with the Royal Society of London, to which, from 1673 until 1723, he communicated by means of informal letters most of his discoveries and to which he was elected a fellow in 1680. His discoveries were for the most part made public in the society's *Philosophical Transactions*. The first representation of bacteria is to be found in a drawing by Leeuwenhoek in that publication in 1683.

His researches on the life histories of various low forms of animal life were in opposition to the doctrine that they could be produced spontaneously or bred from corruption. Thus, he showed that the weevils of granaries (in his time commonly supposed to be bred from wheat as well as in it) are really grubs hatched from eggs deposited by winged insects. His letter on the flea, in which he not only described its structure but traced out the whole history of its metamorphosis, is of great interest, not so much for the exactness of his observations as for an illustration of his opposition to the spontaneous generation of many lower organisms, such as "this minute and despised creature." Some theorists asserted that the flea was produced from sand, others from dust or the like, but Leeuwenhoek proved that it bred in the regular way of winged insects.

Leeuwenhoek also carefully studied the history of the ant and was the first to show that what had been commonly reputed to be ants' eggs were really their pupae, containing the perfect insect nearly ready for emergence, and that the true eggs were much smaller and gave origin to maggots, or larvae. He argued that the sea mussel and other shell-fish were not generated out of sand found at the seashore or mud in the beds of rivers at low water but from spawn, by the regular course of generation. He maintained the same to be true of the freshwater mussel, whose embryos he examined so carefully that he was able to observe how they were consumed by "animalcules," many of which, according to his description, must have included ciliates in conjugation, flagellates, and the Vorticella. Similarly, he investigated the generation of eels, which were at that time supposed to be produced from dew without the ordinary process of generation.

The dramatic nature of his discoveries made him world famous, and he was visited by many notables—including Peter I the Great of Russia, James II of England, and Frederick II the Great of Prussia.

Leeuwenhoek's methods of microscopy, which he kept secret, remain something of a mystery. During his lifetime he ground more than 400 lenses, most of which were very small—some no larger than a pinhead—and usually mounted them between two thin brass plates, riveted together. A large sample of these lenses, bequeathed to the Royal Society, were found to have magnifying powers of between 50 and, at the most, 300 times. In order to observe phenomena as small as bacteria, Leeuwenhoek must have employed some form of oblique illumination, or other technique, for enhancing the effectiveness of the lens, but this method he would not reveal. Leeuwenhoek continued his work almost to the end of his long life of 90 years.

Leeuwenhoek's contributions to the *Philosophical Transactions* amounted to 375 and those to the *Mémoires* of the Paris Academy of Sciences to 27. Two collections of his works appeared during his life, one in Dutch (1685–1718) and the other in Latin (1715–22); a selection was translated by S. Hoole, *The Select Works of A. van Leeuwenhoek* (1798–1807).

Inventors

An era that saw nature as a machine rather than as an organism was bound to bring forth people who were adept in manipulating the materials of the natural world in order to create machines that made work easier and more fruitful. From the printing press to microscopes and telescopes to the first steam engine, these inventions and the men who created them are profiled in this chapter.

JOHANNES GUTENBERG

(b. 14th century, Mainz [Germany]—d. probably Feb. 3, 1468, Mainz)

Johannes Gutenberg (in full Johann Gensfleisch zur Laden zum Gutenberg) was a German craftsman and inventor who originated a method of printing from movable type that was used without important change until the 20th century. The unique elements of his invention consisted of a mold, with punch-stamped matrices (metal prisms used to mold the face of the type) with which type could be cast precisely and in large quantities; a type-metal alloy; a new press, derived from those used in wine making, papermaking, and bookbinding; and an oil-based printing ink. None of these features existed in Chinese or Korean printing, or in the existing European technique of stamping letters on various surfaces, or in woodblock printing.

LIFE

Gutenberg was the son of a patrician of Mainz. What little information exists about him, other than that he had acquired skill in metalwork, comes from documents of financial transactions. Exiled from Mainz in the course of a bitter struggle between the guilds of that city and the patricians, Gutenberg moved to Strassburg (now Strasbourg, France) probably between 1428 and 1430. Records put his presence there from 1434 to 1444. He engaged in such crafts as gem cutting, and he also taught crafts to a number of pupils.

Some of his partners, who became aware that Gutenberg was engaged in work that he kept secret from them, insisted that, since they had advanced him considerable sums, they should become partners in these activities as well. Thus, in 1438 a five-year contract was drawn up between him and three other men: Hans Riffe, Andreas Dritzehn, and Andreas Heilmann. It contained a clause whereby in case of the death of one of the partners, his heirs were not to enter the company but were to be compensated financially.

INVENTION OF THE PRESS

When Andreas Dritzehn died at Christmas 1438, his heirs, trying to circumvent the terms of the contract, began a lawsuit against Gutenberg in which they demanded to be made partners. They lost the suit, but the trial revealed that Gutenberg was working on a new invention. Witnesses testified that a carpenter named Conrad Saspach had advanced sums to Andreas Dritzehn for the building of a wooden press, and Hans Dünne, a goldsmith, declared that he had sold to Gutenberg, as early as 1436, 100 guilders' worth of printing materials. Gutenberg, apparently well along the way to completing his invention, was anxious to keep secret the nature of the enterprise.

After March 12, 1444, Gutenberg's activities are undocumented for a number of years, but it is doubtful that he returned immediately to Mainz, for the quarrel between patricians and guilds had been renewed in that city. In October 1448, however, Gutenberg was back in Mainz to borrow more money, which he received from a relative. By 1450 his printing experiments had apparently reached a considerable degree of refinement, for he was able to persuade Johann Fust, a wealthy financier, to lend him 800 guilders—a very substantial capital investment, for which the tools and equipment for printing were to act as securities. Two years later Fust made an investment of an additional 800 guilders for a partnership in the enterprise. Fust and Gutenberg eventually became estranged, Fust, apparently, wanting a safe and quick return on his investment, while Gutenberg aimed at perfection rather than promptness.

Fust won a suit against him, the record of which is preserved, in part, in what is called the Helmaspergersches Notariatsinstrument (Helmasperger notarial instrument), dated Nov. 6, 1455, now in the library of the University of Göttingen. Gutenberg was ordered to pay Fust the total sum of the two loans and compound interest (probably totaling 2,020 guilders). Traditional historiography suggested that this settlement ruined Gutenberg, but more recent scholarship suggests that it favoured him, allowing him to operate a printing shop through the 1450s and maybe into the 1460s.

PRINTING OF THE BIBLE

There is no reason to doubt that the printing of certain books (*werck der bucher*, specifically mentioned in the record of the trial, refers to the Forty-two-Line Bible that was Gutenberg's masterpiece) was completed, according to Gutenberg's major biographers, in 1455 at the latest. It has been estimated that the sale of the Forty-two-Line Bible alone would have produced many times over the sum owed Fust by Gutenberg, and there exists no explanation as to why these tangible assets were not counted among Gutenberg's property at the trial.

Painting depicting Johannes Gutenberg (far right) *inspecting a page from his printing press.* Rischgitz/Hulton Archive/Getty Images

After winning his suit, Fust gained control of the type for the Bible and for Gutenberg's second masterpiece, a Psalter, and at least some of Gutenberg's other printing equipment. He continued to print, using Gutenberg's materials, with the assistance of Peter Schöffer, his son-in-law, who had been Gutenberg's most skilled employee and a witness against him in the 1455 trial. The first printed book in Europe to bear the name of its printer is a magnificent Psalter completed in Mainz on August 14, 1457, which lists Johann Fust and Peter Schöffer.

The Psalter is decorated with hundreds of two-colour initial letters and delicate scroll borders that were printed in a most ingenious technique based on multiple inking on a single metal block. Most experts are agreed that it would have been impossible for Fust and Schöffer alone to have invented and execute the intricate technical equipment necessary to execute this process between Nov. 6, 1455, when Gutenberg lost control of his printing establishment, and Aug. 14, 1457, when the Psalter appeared. It was Gutenberg's genius that was responsible for the Psalter decorations. In the 1960s it was suggested that he may also have had a hand in the creation of copper engraving, in which he may have recognized a method for producing pictorial matrices from which to cast reliefs that could be set with the type, initial letters, and calligraphic scrolls. It is at present no more than a hypothesis, but Gutenberg's absorption in both copper engraving and the Psalter decorations would certainly have increased Johann Fust's impatience and vindictiveness.

A number of other printings used to be attributed to Gutenberg. They are now considered the work of other minor printers; among these is a Thirty-six-Line Bible printed in Bamberg, a typographic resetting of the Forty-two-Line Bible. Attributed to Gutenberg himself is a *Türkenkalender*, a warning against the impending danger of

Turkish invasion after the fall of Constantinople in 1453, printed December 1454 for 1455 use, some letters of indulgence, and some school grammars. The identity of the printer of a *Missale Speciale Constantiense* is still not established, but it was probably produced about 1473 in Basel, Switzerland.

In January 1465 the archbishop of Mainz pensioned Gutenberg, giving him an annual measure of grain, wine, and clothing and exempting him from certain taxes. His financial status in his last years has been debated but was probably not destitute.

HANS LIPPERSHEY

(b. c. 1570, Wesel, Germany—d. c. 1619, Middelburg, Netherlands)

Hans Lippershey (also called Jan Lippersheim, or Hans Lippersheim) was a spectacle maker from the Netherlands, traditionally credited with inventing the telescope (1608).

Lippershey applied to the States General of the Netherlands for a 30-year patent for his instrument, which he called a *kijker* ("looker"), or else an annual pension, in exchange for which he offered not to sell telescopes to foreign kings. Two other claimants to the invention came forward, Jacob Metius and Zacharias Jansen. The States General ruled that no patent should be granted because so many people knew about it and the device was so easy to copy. However, the States General granted Lippershey 900 florins for the instrument but required its modification into a binocular device. His telescopes were made available to Henry IV of France and others before the end of 1608. The potential importance of the instrument in astronomy was recognized by, among others, Jacques Bovedere of Paris; he reported the invention to Galileo, who promptly built his own telescope.

SIR JOHN HARINGTON AND THE FLUSH TOILET

Sir John Harington (b. 1561—d. Nov. 20, 1612, Kelston, Somerset, England) was an English Elizabethan courtier, translator, author, and wit who also invented the flush toilet.

Harington's father enriched the family by marrying an illegitimate daughter of Henry VIII; his second wife was an attendant to the Princess Elizabeth, who stood as godmother for John. Educated at Eton, Cambridge, and Lincoln's Inn, London, Harington married in 1583. For translating and circulating among the ladies a wanton tale from the 16th-century Italian poet Ariosto, he was banished from court until he should translate the whole of Ariosto's epic poem *Orlando Furioso*. The translation, published in 1591, remains one of the finest of the age.

Probably at that time he invented the flush lavatory (toilet) and installed one for Queen Elizabeth in her palace at Richmond, Surrey. In 1596, in *The Metamorphosis of Ajax* (a jakes; i.e., privy), Harington described his invention in terms more Rabelaisian than mechanical and was again banished by Elizabeth. In 1599 he went on a military expedition to Ireland, winning a knighthood. His barbed epigrams and wanton writings gave too much offense, particularly under James I, to advance him beyond a reputation as Elizabeth's "saucy godson."

CORNELIS DREBBEL

(b. 1572, Alkmaar, Netherlands—d. Nov. 7, 1633, London)

Cornelis Jacobszoon Drebbel was a Dutch inventor who built the first navigable submarine.

An engraver and glassworker in Holland, Drebbel turned to applied science and in 1604 went to England, where King James I became his patron. He devised an ingenious "perpetual motion clock," actuated by changes in atmospheric pressure and temperature, which greatly enhanced his reputation. In 1620 he completed his "diving boat." Propelled by oars and sealed against the water by a covering of greased leather, the wooden vessel traveled the Thames River at a depth of about 12 to 15 feet (4 metres) from Westminster to Greenwich. Air was supplied by two tubes with floats to maintain one end above water.

Drebbel also discovered the use of tin compounds as mordants for cochineal, a scarlet dye, and suggested a method of making sulfuric acid by the oxidation of sulfur. Among many other inventions attributed to him are the compound microscope, an improved thermometer, and self-regulating ovens.

EVANGELISTA TORRICELLI

(b. Oct. 15, 1608, Faenza, Romagna—d. Oct. 25, 1647, Florence)

Evangelista Torricelli was an Italian physicist and mathematician who invented the barometer and whose work in geometry aided in the eventual development of integral calculus. Inspired by Galileo's writings, he wrote a treatise on mechanics, *De Motu* ("Concerning Movement"), which impressed Galileo. In 1641 Torricelli was invited to Florence, where he served the elderly astronomer as secretary and assistant during the last three months of Galileo's life. Torricelli was then appointed to succeed him as professor of mathematics at the Florentine Academy.

Two years later, pursuing a suggestion by Galileo, he filled a glass tube 4 feet (1.2 metres) long with mercury and inverted the tube into a dish. He observed that some of the mercury did not flow out and that the space above the mercury in the tube was a vacuum. Torricelli became the first man to create a sustained vacuum. After much observation, he concluded that the variation of the height of the mercury from day to day was caused by changes in atmospheric pressure. He never published his findings, however, because he was too deeply involved in the study of pure mathematics—including calculations of the cycloid, a geometric curve described by a point on the rim of a turning wheel. In his *Opera Geometrica* (1644; "Geometric Works"), Torricelli included his findings on fluid motion and projectile motion.

OTTO VON GUERICKE

(b. Nov. 20, 1602, Magdeburg, Prussian Saxony [now in Germany]—d. May 11, 1686, Hamburg)

Otto von Guericke was a German physicist, engineer, and natural philosopher who invented the first air pump and used it to study the phenomenon of vacuum and the role of air in combustion and respiration.

Guericke was educated at the University of Leipzig and studied law at the University of Jena in 1621 and mathematics and mechanics at the University of Leyden in 1623. In 1631 he became an engineer in the army of Gustavus II Adolphus of Sweden, and from 1646 to 1681 he was bürgermeister (mayor) of Magdeburg and magistrate for Brandenburg.

In 1650 Guericke invented the air pump, which he used to create a partial vacuum. His studies revealed that light travels through a vacuum but sound does not. In 1654, in a famous series of experiments that were performed before Emperor Ferdinand III at Regensburg, Guericke placed two copper bowls (Magdeburg hemispheres) together to

ICONISMUS XII.

Otto von Guericke's demonstration of the power of air pressure, Regensburg, 1654. A platform was suspended from the bottom of an evacuated sphere made up of two copper hemispheres, and increasing numbers of weights were placed on it. From von Guericke's Experimenta Nova (ut vocantur) Magdeburgica de Vacuo Spatio *("New Magdeburg Experiments About the Vacuum"), 1672.* © Photos.com/Thinkstock

Title page of Experimenta Nova (ut vocantur) Magdeburgica de Vacuo Spatio *("New Magdeburg Experiments About the Vacuum"), 1672, in which Otto von Guericke published details of his invention of the air pump and the power of air pressure.* © Photos.com/Thinkstock

form a hollow sphere about 14 inches (35.5 cm) in diameter. After he had removed the air from the sphere, horses were unable to pull the bowls apart, even though they were held together only by the air around them. The tremendous force that air pressure exerts was thus first demonstrated.

In 1663 he invented the first electric generator, which produced static electricity by applying friction against a revolving ball of sulfur. In 1672 he discovered that the electricity thus produced could cause the surface of the sulfur ball to glow; hence, he became the first man to view electroluminescence. Guericke also studied astronomy and predicted that comets would return regularly from outer space.

GIUSEPPE CAMPANI

(b. 1635, Castel San Felice [Italy]—d. July 28, 1715, Rome, Papal States)

Giuseppe Campani was an Italian optical-instrument maker who invented a lens-grinding lathe.

Of peasant origin, Campani as a young man studied in Rome. There he learned to grind lenses and, with his two brothers, invented a silent night clock that, when presented to Pope Alexander VII, brought him fame. Thereafter, he became a full-time lens grinder for about 50 years, constructing telescopes and lenses for important persons and for the Royal Observatory in Paris. In 1664 he developed his lens-grinding lathe, with which he made superior lenses for telescopes. He also improved telescope tubes, constructing them of wood rather than of cardboard covered with leather; though somewhat unwieldy, these designs proved durable, and wooden telescopes continued in use until the 19th century. With his own instruments he observed the moons of Jupiter and the rings of Saturn in 1664–65. Subsequently, he devised a

screw-barrel microscope that could be adjusted by rotating it within a threaded ring. That device supplanted sliding barrel types held only by friction, permitting far more precise adjustment.

JAMES GREGORY

(b. November 1638, Drumoak [near Aberdeen], Scotland—d. October 1675, Edinburgh)

James Gregory (also spelled James Gregorie) was a Scottish mathematician and astronomer who discovered infinite series representations for a number of trigonometry functions, although he is mostly remembered for his description of the first practical reflecting telescope, now known as the Gregorian telescope.

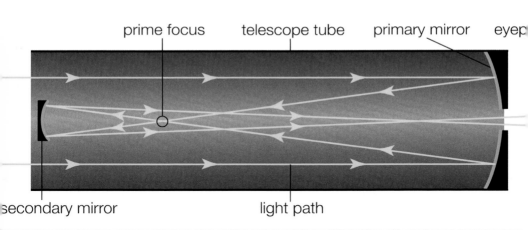

James Gregory's telescope design (1663) uses two concave mirrors—a primary parabolic-shaped mirror and a secondary elliptic-shaped mirror—to focus images in a short telescope tube. As indicated by the yellow rays in the figure: (1) light enters the open end of the telescope; (2) light rays travel to the primary mirror, where they are reflected and concentrated at the prime focus; (3) a secondary mirror slightly beyond the prime focus reflects and concentrates the rays near a small aperture in the primary mirror; and (4) the image is viewed through an eyepiece. Encyclopædia Britannica, Inc.

The son of an Anglican priest, Gregory received his early education from his mother. After his father's death in 1650, he was sent to Aberdeen, first to grammar school and then to Marischal College, graduating from the latter in 1657. (This Protestant college was combined with the Roman Catholic King's College in 1860 to form the University of Aberdeen.)

Following graduation, Gregory traveled to London where he published *Optica Promota* (1663; "The Advance of Optics"). This work analyzed the refractive and reflective properties of lens and mirrors based on various conic sections and substantially developed Johannes Kepler's theory of the telescope. In the epilogue, Gregory proposed a new telescope design with a secondary mirror in the shape of a concave ellipsoid that would collect the reflection from a primary parabolic mirror and refocus the image back through a small hole in the centre of the primary mirror to an eyepiece. In this work Gregory also introduced estimation of stellar distances by photometric methods.

In 1663 Gregory visited The Hague and Paris before settling in Padua, Italy, to study geometry, mechanics, and astronomy. While in Italy he wrote *Vera Circuli et Hyperbolae Quadratura* (1667; "The True Squaring of the Circle and of the Hyperbola") and *Geometriae Pars Universalis* (1668; "The Universal Part of Geometry"). In the former work he used a modification of the method of exhaustion of Archimedes to find the areas of the circle and sections of the hyperbola. In his construction of an infinite sequence of inscribed and circumscribed geometric figures, Gregory was one of the first to distinguish between convergent and divergent infinite series. In the latter work Gregory collected the main results then known about transforming a very general class of curves into sections of known curves (hence the designation "universal"), finding the areas bounded by such curves, and calculating the volumes of their solids of revolution.

On the strength of his Italian treatises, Gregory was elected to the Royal Society on his return to London in 1668 and appointed to the University of St. Andrews, Scotland. In 1669, shortly after his return to Scotland, he married a young widow and started his own family. He visited London only once again, in 1673, to purchase supplies for what would have been Britain's first public astronomical observatory. In 1674, however, he became dissatisfied with the University of St. Andrews and left for the University of Edinburgh.

Although Gregory did not publish any more mathematical papers after his return to Scotland, his mathematical research continued. In 1670 and 1671 he communicated to the English mathematician John Collins a number of important results on infinite series expansions of various trigonometry functions, including what is now known as Gregory's series for the arctangent function:

$$\arctan x = x - x^3/3 + x^5/5 - x^7/7 + \ldots$$

Knowing that the arctangent of 1 is equal to $\pi/4$ led to the immediate substitution of 1 for x in this equation to produce the first infinite series expansion for π. Unfortunately, this series converges too slowly to π for the practical generation of digits in its decimal expansion. Nevertheless, it encouraged the discovery of other, more rapidly convergent infinite series for π.

DENIS PAPIN

(b. Aug. 22, 1647, Blois, France—d. c. 1712, London)

Denis Papin was a French-born British physicist who invented the pressure cooker and suggested the first

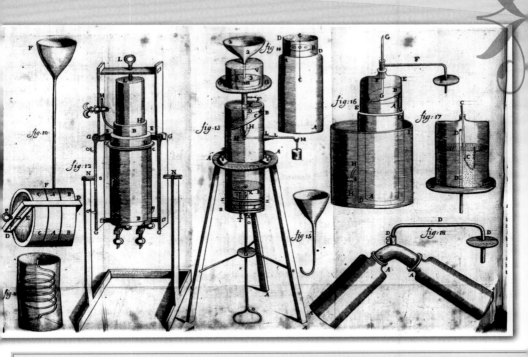

Detailed diagram outlining the mechanics of the pressure cooker, invented by the French-born physicist Denis Papin. Hulton Archive/Getty Images

cylinder and piston steam engine. Though his design was not practical, it was improved by others and led to the development of the steam engine, a major contribution to the Industrial Revolution.

Papin assisted the Dutch physicist Christiaan Huygens with his air-pump experiments and went to London in 1675 to work with the English physicist Robert Boyle. In 1679 Papin invented his steam digester (pressure cooker), a closed vessel with a tightly fitting lid that confines the steam until a high pressure is generated, raising the boiling point of the water considerably. A safety valve of his own invention prevented explosions. Observing that the enclosed steam in his cooker tended to raise the lid, Papin conceived of the use of steam to drive a piston in a cylinder, the basic design for early steam engines; he never built an engine of his own, however.

In 1705 the German physicist and philosopher Gottfried Wilhelm Leibniz sent Papin a sketch of the first practical steam engine, built by Thomas Savery of England. That sketch stimulated Papin to further work, culminating in his *Ars Nova ad Aquam Ignis Adminiculo Efficacissime Elevandam* (1707; "The New Art of Pumping Water by Using Steam"). In 1709 he built a man-powered paddle-wheel boat that successfully demonstrated the practicability of using the paddle wheel in place of oars on steam-driven ships. Later that same year Papin returned to London, where he lived in obscurity until his death.

THOMAS SAVERY

(b. c. 1650, Shilstone, Devonshire, England—d. 1715, London)

Thomas Savery was an English engineer and inventor who built the first steam engine.

A military engineer by profession, Savery was drawn in the 1690s to the difficult problem of pumping water out of coal mines. Using principles adduced by the French physicist Denis Papin and others, Savery patented (1698) a machine consisting of a closed vessel filled with water into which steam under pressure was introduced, forcing the water to a higher level; when the water was expelled, a sprinkler condensed the steam, producing a vacuum capable of drawing up more water through a valve below. To make the effect as nearly continuous as possible, Savery assembled two containing vessels in the same apparatus.

An energetic advertising campaign brought him customers, and he manufactured a number of his engines not only for pumping out mines but also for supplying water to

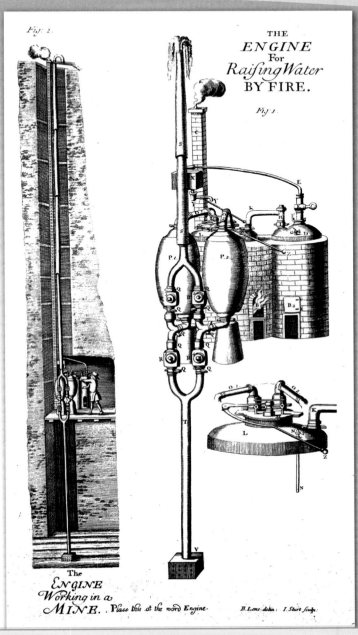

A diagram of the steam pump invented by Thomas Savery. The pump was nicknamed "The Miner's Friend" because the device was first used to pump water out of coal mines. Universal Images Group/Getty Images

large buildings. Savery's engine had many limitations, notably its weakness under high-pressure steam (above 8 to 10 atmospheres). A few years later, when Thomas Newcomen independently designed his atmospheric-pressure piston engine from another of Papin's ideas, Savery, who held patent primacy, joined him in its development. Savery also had other inventions to his credit, including an odometer to measure the distances traveled by ships.

An often overlooked aspect of the Renaissance is the scientific revolution that accompanied it. As with the Renaissance itself, the concept of a revolution in science is complex, having to do with intellectual liberation from the ancient world. For centuries the authority of Aristotle in dynamics, of Ptolemy in astronomy, and of Galen in medicine had been taken for granted. Beginning in the 16th century their authority was challenged by the new heliocentric, mechanistic, and mathematical conceptions of Copernicus, Harvey, Kepler, Galileo, and Newton. Scientists set out by observation and experiment to establish new explanatory models of the natural world.

One distinctive characteristic of these models was that they were tentative, never receiving the authoritarian prestige long accorded to the ancient masters. Historians of science are increasingly reluctant to describe such changes as a revolution, since this implies too sudden and complete an overthrow of the earlier model. Still, the Renaissance made important contributions toward the process of paradigm shift, what the 20th-century historian of science Thomas Kuhn called major innovations in science. Since this fundamental shift of emphasis, science has been committed to a progressive, forward-looking attitude and has come increasingly to seek practical applications for scientific research.

alchemy A theoretical system that involved the effort to change lead into gold.

anatomist A specialist in anatomy.

centripetal Proceeding or acting in a direction toward a centre or axis.

cochineal A red dye made from the dried bodies of the females of a specific scale-covered insect species.

embryology A branch of biology dealing with embryos and their development into fetuses.

geocentric Earth-centred.

heliocentric Sun-centred.

histology A branch of biology studying the organization and makeup of animal and plant tissues.

homeopathy A system of therapy based on the concept that illness-bearing substances have a curative effect when given in very dilute quantities to sick people with a disease caused by the same substances.

humours The four main bodily fluids—blood, yellow bile, black bile, and phlegm linked to ancient diseases and cures.

hydrostatics Branch of physics that deals with the characteristics of fluids at rest, particularly with the pressure in a fluid or exerted by a fluid (gas or liquid) on an immersed body.

iatrophysical Physics combined with medicine, used to teach medical students of the 17th century about disease and the activities of the human body.

immutable Not capable of or susceptible to change.

monolith An organized whole that acts as a single unified powerful or influential force.

mordant Biting and caustic in thought, manner, or style.

perigee The point, in an elliptical Earth orbit, where an object is closest to Earth.

pneumatic Moved or worked by air pressure.

protozoa Members of the subkingdom Protozoa, a collection of single-celled eukaryotic organisms.

refraction Change in a wave's direction caused by its passage through a different medium and the resultant change in the wave's velocity.

supernova A violently exploding star whose luminosity after eruption suddenly increases to many times its normal level.

transmutation The conversion of one element into another, either by natural means or artificially.

vivisection Dissecting or cutting into a live body.

SURVEYS

The vast literature on the scientific revolution is surveyed in H. Floris Cohen, *The Scientific Revolution: A Historiographical Inquiry* (1994). John Henry, *The Scientific Revolution and the Origins of Modern Science*, 3rd ed. (2008); and Steven Shapin, *The Scientific Revolution* (1996), are good short overviews. Lisa Jardine, *Ingenious Pursuits: Building the Scientific Revolution* (1999); and Margaret C. Jacob, *The Cultural Meaning of the Scientific Revolution* (1988, reissued 1993), are strong on comparative and social issues. David C. Lindberg and Robert S. Westman (eds.), *Reappraisals of the Scientific Revolution* (1990), is a collection of essays by historians of science. A. Rupert Hall, *The Revolution in Science, 1500–1750*, 3rd ed. (1983), is a classic intellectual history. Owen Gingerich, *The Eye of Heaven: Ptolemy, Copernicus, Kepler* (1993), is useful for both scholarly and general readers.

BIOGRAPHIES

Popular biographies of Copernicus include Jack Repcheck, *Copernicus' Secret: How the Scientific Revolution Began* (2007); and Dava Sobel, *A More Perfect Heaven: How Copernicus Revolutionized the Cosmos* (2011). Owen Gingerich and James MacLachan, *Nicolaus Copernicus: Making the Earth a Planet* (2005), is for younger readers. Victor E. Thoren, *The Lord of Uraniborg: A Biography of Tycho Brahe* (1990); and John Robert Christianson, *On Tycho's Island: Tycho Brahe and His Assistants, 1570–1601* (2000), are good biographies. An excellent appreciation, for general readers, of Kepler's life and achievements is Owen Gingerich, "Kepler," in Charles Coulston Gillispie (ed.), *Dictionary of Scientific Biography*, vol. 7 (1973), pp. 289–312. Several biographies of Galileo have been written by Stillman Drake: *Galileo at Work: His Scientific Biography* (1978, reissued 1995), *Galileo: Pioneer Scientist* (1990), and *Galileo* (1980). James Reston, Jr., *Galileo* (1994), is a well-documented popular biography.

Noteworthy biographies of Descartes are Geneviève Rodis-Lewis, *Descartes: His Life and Thought* (1998; originally published in French, 1995); John R. Cole, *The Olympian Dreams and Youthful Rebellion of René Descartes* (1992); and Richard A. Watson, *Cogito ergo Sum: The Life of René Descartes* (2002). Richard S. Westfall, *Never at Rest: A Biography of Isaac Newton* (1980, reissued 1990), also available in a shorter version, *The Life of Isaac Newton* (1993), is a comprehensive study of Newton. Gale E. Christianson, *In the Presence of the Creator: Isaac Newton and His Times* (1984), includes much contextual information. Cornelis Dirk Andriesse, *Huygens: The Man Behind the Principle* (2005; originally published in Dutch, 1993), is a thoroughly researched work that is also accessible to the general reader. Rose-Mary Sargent, *The Diffident Naturalist* (1995), discusses Boyle's experimental style and philosophy of science. Lawrence M. Principe, *The Aspiring Adept: Robert Boyle and His Alchemical Quest* (1997), follows Boyle's pursuit of transmutational alchemy.

Franz Hartmann, *The Life of Philippus Theophrastus Bombast of Hohenheim, Known by the Name of Paracelsus, and the Substance of His Teachings* (1887, reprinted in *The Prophecies of Paracelsus*, 1973), is a useful biographical outline, with good translations of extracts from the main works of Paracelsus. C.D. O'Malley, *Andreas Vesalius of Brussels, 1514–1564* (1964), is a complete biography. Jole

Shackelford, *William Harvey and the Mechanics of the Heart* (2003), covers Harvey's life, including his education, his discoveries, and his final years. The definitive study of Malpighi is Howard Adelmann, *Marcello Malpighi and the Evolution of Embryology*, 5 vol. (1966). Two books on van Leeuwenhoek are Clifford Dobell, *Antony van Leeuwenhoek and His "Little Animals"* (1932, reissued 1960); and Brian J. Ford, *Single Lens: The Story of the Simple Microscope* (1985). Two popular biographies of Hooke by authors with scholarly backgrounds are Lisa Jardine, *The Curious Life of Robert Hooke: The Man Who Measured London* (2003); and Stephen Inwood, *The Man Who Knew Too Much: The Strange and Inventive Life of Robert Hooke 1635–1703* (2002).

A

Académie des Sciences, 34, 87,
    89, 135
alchemy, 17, 26, 96, 99, 100, 102
Almagest, 6, 41, 45
Anathomia, 21, 98
anatomy
    human/animal, 20, 21, 28,
        98–99, 106, 107–109,
        110–111, 126, 129, 130
    plant, 28–29, 129, 130
animalcules, 30–32, 133, 134, 135
Aristotle, 9–10, 17, 40, 42, 46, 62,
    63, 66, 70, 73, 76, 83, 96, 100,
    113, 120, 122, 154
Avicenna, 20, 23, 100, 102

B

Bacon, Francis, 27, 114
Bacon, Roger, 15, 117
Banks, Sir Joseph, 18
blood, circulation of, 20, 21, 26–27,
    112, 113, 115, 116–121, 125
Borelli, Giovanni Alfonso,
    24–26, 124, 126, 127
Boyle, Robert, 18, 19–20, 33, 73,
    91, 123, 131, 151
    early life and education, 91–92
    mature years in London, 97
    scientific career, 92–96
    theological activities, 96–97
Boyle's law, 94–95

Brahe, Tycho, 7–8, 35, 44, 55, 58
    mature career, 48–49
    youth and education, 44–46
Brouncker, William, 2nd
    Viscount, 18
Brown, Robert, 118
Browne, Thomas, 24

C

Campani, Giuseppe, 147–148
Canon of Medicine, The, 20
Cassegrain, Laurent, 61
cells, discovery of, 29
*Cerebri Anatome, cui accessit
    Nervorum descriptio et usus*
    ("Anatomy of the Brain, with
    a Description of the Nerves
    and Their Function"), 26, 131
Chauliac, Guy de, 21
Chirurgia magna ("Great
    Surgery"), 21
Christian Virtuoso, The, 97
conservation of momentum and
    of kinetic energy, laws of, 12
Copernicus, Nicolaus, 4, 6–8,
    35–37, 45, 46, 51, 52, 53, 58, 66,
    67, 98, 104, 154
    astronomical work, 39–43
    early life and education, 37–39
    publication of *De revolutionibus*,
        43–44
Copley Medal, 18

D

De contagione et contagiosis morbis,
24, 104

De humani corporis fabrica ("On
the Fabric of the Human
Body"), 21, 98, 109

*De Magnete, Magneticisque
Corporibus et de Magno
Magnete Tellure* ("On the
Magnet, Magnetic Bodies,
and the Great Magnet of the
Earth"), 8, 53

*De Motu Cordis (Exercitatio
Anatomica de Motu Cordis et
Sanguinis in Animalibus /
Anatomical Exercise on the
Motion of the Heart and Blood
in Animals)*, 26–27, 116–118

*De revolutionibus orbium coelestium
libri vi* ("Six Books
Concerning the Revolutions
of the Heavenly Orbs"), 35,
37, 42, 43–44, 52, 67

Descartes, René, 11–12, 14, 15, 16,
24, 37, 58, 73–74, 87, 89
early life and education, 74–76
final years, 80–81
physics, physiology, and
morals, 78–80
residence in the Netherlands, 76
*The World, The Discourse on
Method, and The
Meditations*, 77–78

De Statica Medicina ("On Medical
Measurement"), 24, 113

De venarum ostiolis, 21, 111–112

disease transmission, 24,
104–105

Drebbel, Cornelis, 142–143

E

embryology, 27, 111, 112, 126, 130
Euclid, 15, 53
Euler, Leonhard, 14
*Exercitationes de Generatione
Animalium* ("Exercises on
the Generation of
Animals"), 27, 116

F

Fabrica (De humani corporis fabrica/
"On the Fabric of the
Human Body"), 21, 98, 109
Fabricius, Hieronymus, 21, 26,
111–112, 113
Fallopius, Gabriel, 21, 110–111
flush toilet, invention of, 142
Foscarini, Paolo Antonio, 67
Fracastoro, Girolamo, 23–24,
104–105, 117
Fust, Johann, 33, 138, 139–140

G

Galen, 20, 21, 23, 27, 99, 100, 102,
107, 110, 111, 113, 125, 154
Galileo Galilei, 9, 10–11, 14, 15,
28, 35, 37, 57, 58, 59–62, 77,
112, 130, 141, 143, 154
Copernicanism, 66–70
early life and career, 62–64
the Inquisition, 62, 66, 70–72
telescopic discoveries, 64–66
Gilbert, William, 8, 53
Gregory, James, 61, 148–150
Grosseteste, Robert, 15
Guericke, Otto von, 33, 94,
144–147

Gutenberg, Johannes, 33, 136–137
  invention of the press, 137–138
  life, 137
  printing of the Bible, 139–141

H

Halley, Edmond, 84
Harington, Sir John, 142
Harvey, William, 21, 26–27,
    111–112, 113, 125, 130, 154
  discovery of blood circulation,
    116–121
  education and career, 113–114
  later life, 116
  physician to the king, 114–116
Helmont, Jan Baptista van, 26, 121
  education and early life,
    121–122
  major experiments, 122–123
  other contributions, 123–124
  publications, 122
Hippocrates, 23
Hooke, Robert, 28, 29, 84, 92, 95,
    117, 131–132
Horologium Oscillatorium, 89–90
Huygens, Christiaan, 12, 16–17,
    32, 73, 87–91, 151

I

iatrochemists, 24, 26, 125, 130
iatrophysicists, 24, 112
Ibn al-Haytham (Alhazen), 15

J

Jansen, Hans, 117
Jansen, Zacharias, 117, 141

K

Kepler, Johannes, 4, 8–9, 12, 14, 15,
    35, 37, 49–51, 67, 85, 149, 154
  astronomical work, 52–59
  social world, 51–52

L

Lavoisier, Antoine-Laurent, 123
Leeuwenhoek, Antonie van, 28,
    30–32, 117–118, 132–135
Lippershey, Hans, 60, 117, 141
Locke, John, 92

M

Maestlin, Michael, 51–52, 53, 58
Malpighi, Marcello, 27, 28–29,
    126, 133
  assessment, 130
  life, 126–129
mechanical philosophy, 11
Mémoires, 34, 135
Micrographia, 29, 117, 132
microscopes, invention and
    development of, 28, 29, 30,
    117–118, 119, 133, 143, 148
Mondino dei Liucci, 21, 98–99
Moray, Sir Robert, 18
motion, Newton's three laws of,
    12–14, 85
Müller, Johann, 38

N

Newcomen, Thomas, 154
Newton, Isaac, 12–14, 15, 16, 18,
    34, 37, 49, 51, 61, 73, 81, 90,
    98, 132, 154

early work on motion, 83–84
final years, 86–87
formative influences, 81–83
the *Principia*, 84–86
Newton's rings, 16
Novara, Domenico Maria de, 38

O

Origine of Formes and Qualities, 96
Ortus Medicinae ("Origin of
　Medicine"), 122

P

Papin, Denis, 33, 150–152, 154
Paracelsus, 17, 23, 96, 99, 121, 123
　career, 100–103
　contributions to medicine,
　　103–104
　education, 99–100
Paré, Ambroise, 21–23, 105–106
Pascal, Blaise, 89
Pecham, John, 15
Philosophical Transactions, 18, 34,
　129, 134, 135
Pico della Mirandola, Giovanni,
　38, 40, 41
planetary motion, 4–6, 8–9, 11, 14,
　40–41, 49–51, 52–55, 58, 84
Plato, 4, 8
preformation, 30
*Principia (Philosophiae Naturalis
　Principia Mathematica/
　Mathematical Principles of
　Natural Philosophy)*, 12, 81,
　84–86, 87, 90
printing, development of, 33,
　137–141

Ptolemy, 4–6, 7, 27, 38, 40, 41,
　45, 154

R

Rheticus, Georg Joachim, 37, 38,
　42, 43–44
Royal Society of London,
　18–19, 29, 34, 87, 90, 91, 92,
　97, 117, 127–129, 131, 134,
　135, 150

S

saggiatore, Il (The Assayer)
　68–69
Santorio Santorio, 24, 112–113
Savery, Thomas, 33, 152–154
Sceptical Chymist, The, 96
Schöffer, Peter, 33, 140
scientific societies, start of, 34
spontaneous generation, 32, 122,
　133, 134
steam engine/power, 32, 33, 136,
　150–151, 152–154
surgery, 21–23, 105–106
Sylvius, Franciscus, 26, 124–125
Syphilis sive morbus Gallicus
　("Syphilis or the French
　Disease"), 23, 104

T

telescopes, invention and
　development of, 9, 28, 32, 44,
　57, 60–61, 64, 89, 132, 136,
　141, 147, 148, 149
Torricelli, Evangelista, 143–144

U

universe
    geocentric theory/Ptolemaic
        system, 3–6, 7–8, 10
    heliocentric theory/Copernican
        system, 4, 6–9, 35–37, 38,
        42, 46, 49, 51, 52, 58, 62,
        66, 67, 69, 70, 77, 154

V

Vanini, Lucilio, 76

Vesalius, Andreas, 21, 98, 99,
    106, 111
    assessment, 110
    career, 109–110
    education, 106–107
    the *Fabrica*, 107–109
Viviani, Vincenzo, 63, 72

W

Wilkins, John, 18, 92
Willis, Thomas, 26, 130–131
Wiseman, Richard, 24
Wren, Christopher, 18, 26, 92